IMPLEMENTING

E-Learning

Here Is How You Can

- Manage the Change to E-Learning

- Successfully Market to Learners

- Create an Implementation Strategy

Linking People,
Learning & Performance

Jay Cross and
Lance Dublin

10   09   08   07   06   2   3   4   5   6

ASTD Press is an internationally renowned source of insightful and practical information on workplace learning and performance topics, including training basics, evaluation and return-on-investment (ROI), instructional systems development (ISD), e-learning, leadership, and career development.

Ordering information: Books published by ASTD Press can be purchased by visiting our website at store.astd.org or by calling 800.628.2783 or 703.683.8100.

Library of Congress Control Number: 2002105498

ISBN-10: 1-56286-333-9
ISBN-13: 978-1-56286-333-3

Contents

Preface vii

1. **New Rule, Old Rules, What Rules to Apply** 1
   "If You Build It..." 1
   Spending Does Not Equal Learning 3
   Strategy Is the Key to Success 3
   The Finishing Touch for Your E-Learning 4
   The Companion Website 5
   Your Turn 5

2. **Understanding Change and Marketing Fundamentals** 9
   Fundamentals of Making Business Decisions 10
   Fundamentals of Change Management 12
   Fundamentals of Consumer Marketing 22
   Your Turn 27

3. **Preparing for Successful Implementation** 29
   Organizations Are Systems 30
   The Systems Approach for Implementing E-Learning 31
   Culture Always Wins 31
   Ready, Set, Go! 33
   Leaders Come in All Shapes and Sizes 35
   Losing Faith in E-Learning 39
   On Your Way to Success 39
   Your Turn 40

4. **Really Communicate** 41
   Vision 41
   Mission 42
   Project Identity 42
   Change Communication Plan 43
   Guiding Principles 44
   Determining What to Communicate 45
   Your Turn 46

5. **Analyzing the Environment of the Marketplace**............47
    Research Methods............47
    Elements of Your Market Research 49
    Assembling Your Findings 57
    Your Turn 59

6. **Applying Marketing Design** 61
    The Design Discipline............61
    The Elements of Marketing Design 61
    Put It All Together............78
    Your Turn............79

7. **Launching Your E-Learning Marketing and Implementation Plan** 85
    Customer Wants and Needs and Motivation............85
    Remove the Obstacles to Learning 86
    Getting Learners to Remember............87
    Thinking for the Longer Term 87
    Promotion 88
    Communicating Your Message 89
    Job Aids 93
    Tips 93
    Measuring Success 94
    Your Turn............95

8. **Practical Advice for the E-Learning Marketer** 97
    Writing Effective Advertising Copy 97
    How to Ignite Buzz............98
    Create Direct Mail and Email 99
    How to Sell E-Learning 100
    Your Turn............102

9. **Sustaining Your Marketing and Implementation Efforts**............105
    Keeping Your E-Learning Customers............105
    How Happy Are Your E-Learning Customers? 106
    Making Learning Fun 106
    Respect the Learner 107
    Celebrating Your E-Learning Success............107
    Let the Learners Participate 108
    Maintaining Your E-Learning Edge 108
    Building a Learning Community 109
    Making E-Learning Part of Your Culture............109

Continue to Communicate...110
Pull the Right Levers 111
Your Turn..112

10. Taking Action...115
A Place in History..115
Your E-Learning Implementation Source Document.........117
Refining Your Action Plan 117
Presenting Your Action Plan 118
Just Do It! 119
Your Turn..119

Glossary 133

References 137

About the Authors 139

Preface

Congratulations! You have already planned, sold, designed, and developed or acquired some great e-learning to meet the training and performance needs of your organization. E-learning, as you already know, has the potential to meet exactly the learning needs of your people. But, this promise can only be fulfilled if they understand what you are offering them, are prepared to embark on the e-learning journey, and are willing—even eager—to buy in. Here is where this book and the tried-and-true principles of marketing and change management are valuable.

Ensuring Your Return on Your E-Learning Investment

Now, how can you make sure your organization is ready, willing, and able to not only support your e-learning, but embrace it? And, how can you make sure that your audience knows about and uses your e-learning for the business and performance purposes you intend? This book can serve as your personal guide to building a powerful implementation and marketing strategy for your e-learning. Without this effort, on-target, exciting e-learning initiatives will fall far short of their goals.

Here are some cautionary tales that reveal what can happen without proper e-learning marketing and change management:

- A large bank licensed a multimillion dollar library of e-learning programs; a year later, not a single individual had completed a course!
- A multinational firm built a two-year master's-level curriculum tailored to the needs of its managers; only two managers had taken the program when it was scrapped.
- A chemical firm commissioned a $200,000+ custom course of study to improve its financial operations; management scrapped the program for political reasons.
- A company purchased all-employee library cards for more than a thousand Web-delivered titles; only 5 to 10 percent of eligible staff took even one course.

MARKETING YOUR E-LEARNING

In this book, you will learn how to think like a marketing pro to generate an awareness of your e-learning brand among internal and external customers. You will learn how to build buzz around your e-learning products that translates into successful and well-attended e-learning events. Most important, this book will show you how to position well-designed, performance-enhancing e-learning in a way that keeps the learner and your organization coming back for more.

PREPARING YOUR ORGANIZATION FOR E-LEARNING

Of course, asking your learners to learn in a different way can create anxiety, fear, and resistance in the learners themselves as well as in your organization as a whole. Too few books on e-learning tackle this challenge. In this book you also will learn how to think like a change management practitioner. You will learn how to prepare your organization for the change that is e-learning. You will learn how to develop and implement an effective, two-way communication program. And, most important, this book will show you how to not only prepare your organization for e-learning but also sustain organizational commitment to e-learning over time.

WHY THE FAILURES?

There are many reasons for e-learning failures. Some organizations fail because they don't adequately prepare for major change. Make no mistake about it; implementing a top-to-bottom e-learning system is tough—as tough as installing an enterprise resource planning (ERP) system. It takes planning, leadership, accountability, communications, and commitment.

Some companies have everything in alignment—except the learners. The organization assumes that it knows what's good for the learners, but it's wrong. Think of learners as customers. They need to be sold on e-learning.

Einstein said that you cannot solve a problem while confined by the assumptions that gave rise to the problem in the first place. You can't assume that e-learning will be embraced by the learners. You can't assume that you can implement e-learning in the absence of change management. You can't assume that you are going to solve your e-learning problems by tweaking content and delivery.

This book is for training and performance managers, executives, and training departments who want to make sure that the effort expended to create great e-learning is rewarded with real business results. It will show you how to build solid customer relationships with executives, managers, and learners just as your organization tries to build positive relationships with its customers. It will give you the tools to create a positive image for your e-learning and position it for the greatest success. It will guide you through the process of harnessing organizational support and developing organizational commitment. Furthermore, this book will enable you to ensure your organization realizes its return on its learning investment.

ACKNOWLEDGMENTS

This book would not have been possible without the generous contributions of many individuals and their organizations. Join us in thanking:

Desirée Aragon, SkillSoft
Tom Barron, SRI Consulting—Business Intelligence
Laurie Bennet, Intel Corporation
David Bennett, Parachute Associates
George Brennan, NCRCorporation
Marcia Conner, Learnativity
Linda Galloway, Apollo Associates
Dan Gillis, Hershey Foods
Larry Green, Novartis International AG
Yeoh Phee Guan, The Knowledge House
Rob Harris, Hewlett-Packard
Chuck Hickman, BMW Financial Services
Dan Hiltz, Convergys Corporation
David Holcolme, E-Learning Guild
Keith Irwin, Wells Fargo & Company
Peter Isackson, Tri-Learning
Chuck Jones, Centra
Tom Kelly, Cisco Systems
Laura Keziah, Compass Bank
Karen Kocher, IBM
Claudia L'Amoreaux, Edge-u-cation and Meta-Learning Lab
Peg Maddocks, Cisco Systems
Deborah Masten, JC Penney Company
Beat Meyer, Novartis International AG
Reiner Neumann, Consultant in Change
Don O'Guin, Pharmacia
Clark Quinn, Ottersurf and Meta-Learning Lab
Christina Raes, Raes & Associates
Norbert Reichert, ZF Friedrichshafen

Marc J. Rosenberg, DiamondCluster International
Corina Sanders, Cisco Systems
Susan Schwartz, The River Birch Group
Khalid Shaikh, PeopleSoft
Sandeep Sood, Deep Sun
Deborah Stone, DLS Group
Brenda Sugrue, eLearnia
John Talanca, Novartis International AG
Stu Tanquist, Express Learning
Beth Thomas, The Limited
Eilif Trondsen, SRI Consulting—Business Intelligence
Kara Underwood, Aspect Communications
Ellen Wagner, Learnativity and Meta-Learning Lab
Claudia Welss, Meta-Learning Lab
Kevin Wheeler, Global Learning Resources

We wish you the best of luck!

Jay Cross and Lance Dublin
October 2002

1

New Rule, Old Rules, What Rules to Apply

Today's business operates in a real-time world where innovation rules, competitors appear from all corners, and knowledge provides more leverage than capital. The old rules no longer apply. Traditional approaches to training the corporate workforce are time-consuming and excruciatingly slow. Old-style, trickle-down training with its one-style-fits-all approach simply cannot keep pace. That is what makes e-learning so exciting to so many people.

E-learning keeps people at the top of their game. It leverages technology in new and powerful ways to develop enthusiastic and skilled people. At some companies, e-learning has radically improved productivity, fueled innovation, reduced administrative overhead, inspired employees, accelerated the internal flow of intellectual capital, and built competitive advantage.

But, to make e-learning work, you must address three vital questions:

- What can you do to prepare the learners and the organization in the first place?
- How do you make sure they actually participate?
- How do you keep the learners—and the organization—coming back for more?

"IF YOU BUILD IT . . ."

In the movie *Field of Dreams,* a voice in a cornfield tells the Kevin Costner character, "If you build it, he will come."[*] He takes this to mean that if he creates a baseball diamond on his farm, the ghosts of Shoeless Joe Jackson and seven other Chicago White Sox players banned from the game for throwing the 1919 World Series will show up to play.

1

The Cold, Hard Truth

Let's follow a group of new hires who are taking an e-learning course to be customer service representatives. What outcomes might you expect?

- 30 percent don't even register or begin "compulsory" e-learning (ASTD and the MASIE Center, 2001).
- 20 percent experience technical difficulty (computer virus, poor connectivity, "blue screen of death," no headset, and so on).
- 10 percent are interrupted while trying to work at their desks and never return.
- 20 percent hit a roadblock in the material they cannot overcome, and no email response is received to their query within a day, causing them to drop out in frustration.
- 20 percent drop out because the content is irrelevant or redundant.
- 20 percent drop out because learning is a low priority compared to "real work." (Managers too often reinforce this notion.)
- 30 percent of what might be learned is squandered because people have not learned how to learn.
- 50 percent of what learning remains atrophies before being put into use.

So, who's left? 70% × 80% × 90% × 80% × 80% × 80% × 70% × 50% = 9%. *Less than a tenth cross the finish line.* Your job is to anticipate and overcome these obstacles to implementing e-learning. You reverse-engineer the problems to arrive at their solutions.

In a 2001 survey, ASTD and the MASIE Center asked of e-learning, "If we build it, will they come?" The study found that many of the potential attendees do not come. According to the report, "the average start rate for courses where participation was voluntary was a mere 32 percent, significantly lower than mandatory courses. However, mandatory courses were far from perfect as well, averaging only a 69 percent start rate." And, that's a typical story.

The ASTD/MASIE study found that "full participation tended to occur when courses:

- had an internal champion
- were tied to performance reviews
- were NOT taken at the desk
- had intense marketing and promotion."

The study recommends these best practices to increase e-learning participation and satisfaction:

- Use intentional, dynamic, and continuous marketing activities, as well as traditional marketing methods, such as face-to-face discussions and print advertising.
- Create a learning culture: encourage and show appreciation of e-learning.

■ Develop an environment in which peer support is endemic.
■ Develop incentive programs, such as job ladders and peer recognition, that go beyond candy bars and meaningless certificates.

If you are not getting full value out of e-learning, don't blame the training department, the corporate information technology department, line managers, trainers, or employees. E-learning is a new way of enabling, extending, and enhancing learning. It requires not only new technologies, but also new ways of working, new relationships, new frameworks, and new priorities. *Implementing E-Learning* will guide you through this maze of new concepts. It will help you prepare, launch, and sustain successful e-learning in your organization by applying change management from the top and consumer marketing principles from the bottom.

Spending Does Not Equal Learning

Despite the promise of e-learning, some corporations are pouring hundreds of millions of dollars into it and receiving little in return. For some, e-learning has become a reprise of the debacle last decade when truckloads of training CD-ROMs made their way from suppliers to training departments to dumpsters, untouched by learners' hands.

E-learning may become the best productivity booster of all time, but, in many cases, e-learning has not lived up to its promises (table 1-1). If employees don't participate, they receive no benefit. If e-learning fails to significantly change their behavior and their on-the-job performance, the organization doesn't benefit.

Corporate decision makers have a choice. They can throw e-learning out the door and risk eroding their human capital. Or, they can fix what's wrong and join the ranks of high-performing, flexible, knowledgeable 21st-century companies that embrace e-learning through change management and effectively market their e-learning to generate excitement about it among potential learners.

Strategy Is the Key to Success

E-learning that does not change employee performance to support corporate objectives is not working. If you want to build an implementation strategy that works for your e-learning, you will need to stay focused on the following items:

■ *Processes that have worked in other settings:* Which approaches have worked in organizations similar to yours? Which approaches have you used for other clients?
■ *The business goals of the organization:* Where is the organization going? Who are the stakeholders and what are their concerns?

Table 1-1. Promises and realities of e-learning.

Promise of E-Learning	Reality
E-learning is a powerful way for people to learn.	As many as half of potential e-learners never show up.
Learners will love the convenience of any-time, anywhere learning.	Learners sometimes perceive e-learning as just one more thing to squeeze into a busy day.
People can learn at their desks, taking advantage of slack periods.	Continual interruptions make the office a poor environment for learning. Workers no longer have slack time.
E-learning is simply a better, faster, cheaper way to train.	Effective e-learning is a major change that requires support from all levels.
Employees will readily embrace e-learning as a better way to get the job done.	Employees must be sold on "what's in it for me" or they will not participate.

- *Barriers to change:* How can you identify barriers that exist in your organization? How can you remove them?
- *The individual learner:* How can you make each learner a partner in the progress of the company? What can you do to promote effective learning? How can you convert learners into enthusiastic fans?
- *Change management:* How can you empower management? What do you need to do to prepare the organization and learners for e-learning? What organizational changes are needed to sustain e-learning after the initial launch?

THE FINISHING TOUCH FOR YOUR E-LEARNING

This book is the capstone volume in a series of books on e-learning published by ASTD. The other books in the series—*Designing E-Learning, Selling E-Learning, Using E-Learning, Evaluating E-Learning,* and *Leading E-Learning*—provide the foundation for *Implementing E-Learning.*

This book is not a cookbook. It is more a general guide to help you successfully implement e-learning in your organization by applying proven techniques and approaches from change management and consumer marketing. Each chapter builds upon the next as you create an e-learning marketing and implementation program that works for you.

Each chapter concludes with Your Turn exercises for you to complete. By the time you finish the book you'll have a change management and marketing document with which to go forward.

In the first four chapters, you'll build a cover memo documenting these issues:

- what you need to do, background (chapter 1)
- reasons behind marketing and branding (chapter 2)
- organizational culture and change (chapter 3)
- a vision and mission for e-learning, as well as a communication summary (chapter 4).

In the next five chapters, you'll develop a marketing and implementation plan by assembling these components:

- market research, industry analysis, current brand image (chapter 5)
- an elevator pitch and action strategy (chapter 6)
- a launch plan (chapter 7)
- draft brochure, poster, email, and promotional materials (chapter 8)
- sustainment and renewal plan (chapter 9).

In the final chapter, you'll put together the pieces to create an implementation action plan for your e-learning.

THE COMPANION WEBSITE

Implementing e-learning is too large a topic to fit between the covers of any book. For additional examples, processes, stories, and other new material, visit the companion Website (www.InternetTime.com), where you will find a Center of Implementation Excellence. Also available on the site are planning forms, promotional materials, media plans, sample campaigns, marketing graphics, and more. You can join in online discussions of implementation issues. Have a question about implementing e-learning? The Website is the place to ask it. Conducted a campaign you're particularly proud of? Submit it to be included on the site.

YOUR TURN

If you are a training and performance professional, you've no doubt heard and read much about the promises of e-learning, and it is likely that you've heard—

or experienced—some e-learning horror stories. Using worksheet 1-1, create a table similar to table 1-1 to contrast the promises of e-learning against the realities for your organization.

Worksheet 1-1. The promises and realities of e-learning in your organization.

Promise of E-Learning	Reality

If you have designed an e-learning program and are now ready to implement it (or you are thinking ahead and planning how to implement a proposed program), what is your gut instinct about the challenges you will face? Using worksheet 1-2 as a guide, take a look at factors within your organization that may help or hinder your implementation. How many good signs do you see and what are they? And, what are the bad signs you need to watch out for or plan to address?

Worksheet 1-2. Organizational influences on your e-learning implementation plans.

Read the list of organizational influences, and then circle the good sign or bad sign that seems to prevail at your organization. There's space to add other items at the bottom so that you can customize the list as needed.

Organizational Influence	Good Sign	Bad Sign
Major new initiative such as merger, ERP implementation, new product launch	Management sees e-learning as integral to the project	Project team to do "its own training"
Perceived value of e-learning	Delivers business results, increases intellectual capital	Is viewed merely as a way to cut costs and training headcounts
Supervisor attitude toward learning	E-learning is a component of every knowledge worker's job	E-learning can't interfere with getting the job done: "Let them do it at home"
Prior e-learning experience	Last year's e-learning was concise, on-target, well received, and effective	Last year's e-learning was bloated, off-base, and boring; drop-out rates were off the charts

* *Field of Dreams.* (1989). Directed by Phil Alden Robinson, written by W.P. Kinsella (book) and Phil Alden Robinson (screenplay).

2

Understanding Change and Marketing Fundamentals

". . . The 'soft stuff' is really hard stuff. I used to believe that, in organizational change, issues such as human resources were fluffy and insubstantial, an afterthought. The only things that I believed mattered were technology and hard design. I've learned that what I considered hard or difficult is, in fact, the 'easy stuff.' The technology issues are the easiest to deal with and don't usually make the most difference."

Michael Hammer (April, 1990)

Authentic marketing is ". . . not the art of selling what you make but knowing what to make. It is the art of identifying and under-standing customer needs and creating solutions that deliver satisfaction to the customers, profits to the producers and bene-fits for the stakeholders."

Philip Kotler (1999)

Effective implementation of e-learning requires understanding and expertise in three areas:

- business decision making
- change management
- consumer marketing.

This chapter will ground you in the basics of these areas.

FUNDAMENTALS OF MAKING BUSINESS DECISIONS

Several years ago, a researcher told three or four dozen training managers how to sell their programs by using return-on-investment (ROI) calculations. The attendee suggested they:

1. Get cost figures from the finance department.
2. Calculate savings in travel cost, salaries, and facilities.
3. Tote up the value of improved performance after the training.
4. Divide the benefits by the costs.

Presto! The training managers could whip out convincing ROI numbers to back up their budget requests and justify the proposed training. Right? Wrong! Wise managers know that ROI numbers are no better than the assumptions they are based on and that assumptions are often fantastically overoptimistic. Certainly ROI is a hurdle every project over a certain size must clear, but it's not compelling on its own. It certainly is not enough to sell management on the value of an e-learning project.

Think Business

To get management on board, you must think like a businessperson. Consider that the overarching focus of business leaders is creating value for stakeholders, including owners, managers, workers, partners, and outside customers. The firm's leaders are responsible for articulating a vision of how the organization will create value and for specifying milestone objectives along the way. Any businessperson worthy of the name can show how his or her activities support those objectives and help fulfill the vision. You, too, must be able to articulate how e-learning establishes value in these areas.

Analytical and Decision-Making Techniques

Here are techniques for business analysis and decision making that should help you as you implement your e-learning. Run through these techniques whenever you are making major decisions until they become second nature to you.

Trade-off. Every business decision is a trade-off. (If there's no trade-off, there's really no decision to be made.) List the pros and cons of the alternatives you are weighing. Try to be aware of what you're trading off when making a decision.

Risk. Every decision is made with less-than-perfect information, and every decision entails taking a risk. The way to make sound decisions is to judge when you have enough information to move ahead and when the level of risk is acceptable. A decision maker who takes no risk receives no reward. A decision maker who disregards risk is a fool, a pauper, or both. Financial decisions trade off risk and reward. Make sure your upside reward outweighs your downside risk.

Empathy. To understand your customers, walk a mile in their shoes. Here's how: Make up several representative customers (personas). Give them names, positions, preferences, gripes, habits, intelligence, and personalities. When you're planning marketing campaigns and learning activities, stop every now and again to slip into these personas' shoes. How does your proposal make them feel?

Inputs and Outputs. The Pareto Principle, also known as the 80/20 rule, describes the common situation where 20 percent of the effort achieves 80 percent of the results. It's not uncommon for 20 percent of the salesforce to make 80 percent of the sales, or for 20 percent of the customers to generate 80 percent of the profits. It's likely that 20 percent of your effort produces 80 percent of your results. The point is that input and output are not balanced. Marketers break the market into pieces, or segments, to identify and focus their attention on the significant few who produce most of the results.

For designers of learning experiences, less is often more. Find the elusive 20 percent of the learner's time that yields 80 percent of what is learned and put your energies there.

The Bottom Line. Revenue minus costs equals profit. Over time, profit and shareholder value are the same thing. The total value of the shares is equivalent to the stream of expected future profits, discounted for the cost of capital. You must be able to relate your decisions and choices to the profitability of your organization. Otherwise, you will not be able to make sound decisions as conditions change.

A Core Focus. Shareholder value (also known as the market cap) is a function of sustained competitive advantage, and organizations achieve it by leveraging their core competencies. Focus on core; outsource everything else. Everything else is context (overhead), and context is a needless distraction. Without careful management, context *always* gets in the way of core because it absorbs time, talent, and management attention (Moore, 2000).

Business leaders present themselves to the world as confident, authoritative, conservative, results-oriented, deliberate, and a bit staid. It's best to leave your clown suit in the closet when you're selling an e-learning concept to executives. Be concise. Hit the concepts described above as they apply to your project. When you've said your piece, ask for questions and sit down.

FUNDAMENTALS OF CHANGE MANAGEMENT

Change? @#%$@#! Hate it. Deny it. Hide from it. Embrace it. It really doesn't matter because change will happen anyway. You have to live with changes in age, weight, hair color, likes and dislikes, interests, relationships, jobs, homes, cars, music, and bosses. Some change you may initiate and feel in control of, and other change happens to you over which you have little control. Some change you may like and some change you don't.

It is the rare individual who awakens each morning thinking "I can hardly wait to find out what changes are in store for me today!" Most people are content to get caught up with work, finish what they've started, still have a job, and know what it is.

With each change there is danger that things won't turn out the way you expect, that this is a crisis. As a matter of fact, the Chinese ideograph for *crisis* incorporates the characters representing *danger* and *opportunity*. But, every time there is a change there is also the opportunity for something new to happen—something better, easier, more productive, more effective, even transformational.

For organizations, adapting to change poses particularly complex challenges. Because the successful functioning of an organization depends on the interaction and cooperation of many different units, a change made in one area will almost certainly necessitate change in other areas. This systems effect requires that change be coordinated throughout the organization to minimize disruptions and to produce the desired effects.

In other words, positive adaptation to change—including implementation of e-learning—requires taking stock of the changing environment, deciding how to adapt to it, making a logical plan of action, and forging ahead. That's change management. And, not only must an organization manage change, but it must also ensure that the desired business impact from the change is, in fact, achieved.

The bottom line, though, is the fact that organizations don't change, people do! The human factor is an unpredictable variable in the change process because human beings instinctually resist change. They rarely embrace every new idea or change in their environments. Humans want to know, "What does this mean to me?" They want to know, to see, to feel, to touch, to have their fears addressed and questions answered before lending support to a new endeavor, to a new way of doing things.

Technology-Based Change

Changes in technology or changes that include technology can provoke extreme responses from employees, ranging from open, unqualified support ("All right! We should have done this years ago! Sign me up!") to blatant, unqualified resistance ("There's no way I'm going to do this!") to subversive resistance ("I'm not doing that, and I'm not going to tell them!"). Between these extreme reactions lie myriad human responses to organizational change, some of which may include: "I'll wait and see." "Who's behind this and what are they up to?" "I'm not sure yet. Show me." "Will I lose my job?" "This will never work." "We've heard this 100 times before and nothing ever came of it." "I'm afraid of this." "We've tried this before and it failed."

E-learning certainly qualifies as a significant technology change, and, so, may provoke any or all of these reactions. Learners used to human contact might resent having to interact with a computer screen. Trainers who are valued for their platform skills might feel threatened. And, managers who have controlled access to training might feel undermined when learners can access courses and learning resources anytime, anywhere.

Organizationally, the effect of these individual responses may be experienced as lack of participation, high dropout rates, and conflict between units and staff, among others. Such backlashes can doom your e-learning project to failure.

Models for Understanding Change

As you might well imagine, there already exists a tremendous body of knowledge about change. Visit your local library or search the Internet, and you'll come across more theories and examples and models than you could ever digest and apply in a lifetime. The following sections describe a few select models of change that can be helpful in planning for and implementing e-learning.

The Transition Landscape. "It isn't the changes that do you in, it's the transitions," according to William Bridges, noted authority on change and change management. Bridges (1991) identifies three stages in the transition process: endings, the neutral zone, and beginnings (figure 2-1).

It should come as no surprise that every change begins with an ending; something that once was exists no more. Typically, people fight endings and try to hang onto the past.

As people begin to let go of the past, they enter a neutral zone. The future seems unclear, and people aren't sure just how to feel, what to do, or how to act. Some people compare the neutral zone to being in a fog or a cloud. The only way through is to keep going.

Remember that for every ending there is also a new beginning. This is the start of the next new phase, which may feel uncomfortable and strange at first, but over time people get used to it.

Your e-learning implementation will go through these same stages. Initially, it will be seen as the end of instructor-led training and all that that has meant. Learners, trainers, and managers may be inclined to try to hold onto

Figure 2-1. Bridges's model of transitions.

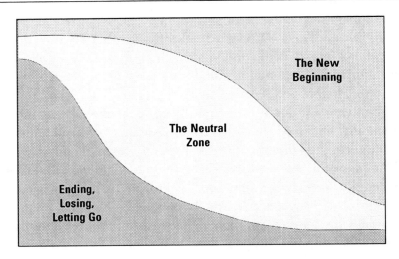

Source: Adapted from Bridges, W. (1991). *Managing Transitions: Making the Most of Change*. Reading, MA: Addison-Wesley Publishing Company.

the old way of doing things. But, as your implementation proceeds, they will begin to let go of this past and will be open to exploring what e-learning can offer to them. A well-designed implementation strategy will give them confidence and support while they are in their neutral zone. And, most important, your implementation strategy will set stage for their future with e-learning and the new beginning it represents.

Making Transitions. Because change is really about people, understanding how they respond to change is critical. Jaffe and Scott (1995) lay out an excellent model based on their work as psychologists and the work of the noted psychiatrist Elisabeth Kubler-Ross (figure 2-2).

The first stage is denial, a refusal to accept that a change is really happening. The key to this phase is that denial remains largely under the surface and rarely is expressed outwardly. People usually are not even aware that they are in denial.

The second stage is resistance, in which people emerge from the trauma of denial and start the process of letting go of the past. Many excuses are made for not changing. During this stage, some people may experience anger and depression. This stage represents a bottoming out of the change process. It's the point where people cross the line and begin to move toward commitment and a more external focus (figure 2-3).

Figure 2-2. The four stages of change.

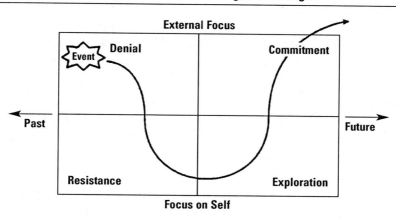

Source: Reprinted with permission from Jaffe, D., and C. Scott. (1995). *Managing Change at Work: Leading People Through Organizational Transitions* (revised edition). Menlo Park, CA: Crisp Publications.

At some point in the transition process, people stop feeling bad, helpless, angry, and confused. They begin to focus on how to meet the challenges brought on by the change and begin to accept it. They start to look more forward than backward. They start to explore how the change will affect them, how things will be different and feel different. This exploration stage is positive and

Figure 2-3. The effect of organizational forces and time on resistance and stress levels.

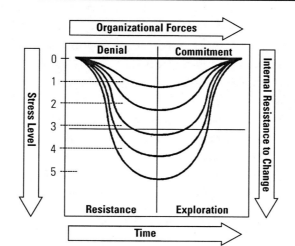

Source: Reprinted with permission from Jaffe, D., and C. Scott. (1995). *Managing Change at Work: Leading People Through Organizational Transitions* (revised edition). Menlo Park, CA: Crisp Publications.

exciting. However, this portion of the transition is not as simple as it sounds, as people tend to zigzag between resistance and exploration.

Finally, people enter the last stage, commitment. They become committed to new ways of working, thinking, and being. They settle into new patterns and behaviors. It's time to celebrate, while realizing at the same time that change is a continuous process. The next change event lies just ahead, and the transition journey begins all over again.

Learners making the transition to e-learning will find themselves going through all of these phases: denial, resistance, confusion, exploration, and commitment. New e-learners might, at first, just refuse to try at all. They then might find ways to avoid your e-learning by dropping out, losing their passwords, forgetting the procedures, and complaining about what they find—all the while saying that it's not their fault it doesn't seem to work.

A well-designed implementation strategy can ensure that learners are supported through the early phases and enable them to explore what e-learning can offer them that is positive. Communications at this time are critical. Encouragement, success stories, and person-to-person support are necessary so that learners don't let their frustrations and discomfort with a new way overwhelm them. Over time—and it will take time—learners will experience the benefits for themselves. They will become comfortable with e-learning. It will become a part of their everyday life, and, then, watch out because you won't be able to take it away from them!

Phases of Organizational Change

How do you get an organization as a whole to commit to change? Daryl Conner (1993) defines three specific phases in the organization's commitment process: preparation, acceptance, and commitment (figure 2-4).

Two stages constitute the preparation phase: contact and awareness. Contact is when people first hear about or find out about the change. Results of this phase can either be unawareness or awareness. It goes without saying which is better. Once people move into awareness, the possible outcomes are confusion and understanding. Again, it's obvious which is necessary for success.

The acceptance phase follows. People now develop an understanding of the nature, intent, and scope of the change. Once aware, they are able to judge it, and based on this judgment—positive or negative—they act or react accordingly. Even if people perceive the change to be positive, they still have to decide whether they are going to support it. Support is necessary to pass through the "commitment threshold."

Conner's final phase is commitment. But, even if this point is reached, the final outcome is still uncertain. Initially the focus is operational in nature; the

---

Figure 2-4. Conner's stages of change commitment.

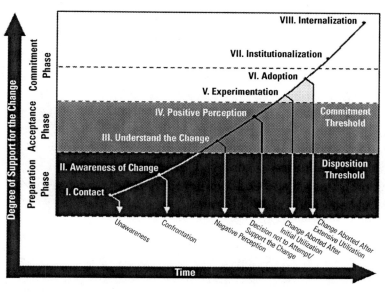

Source: Reprinted with permission from ODR.

goal is to install the change. Installation focuses on the nuts and bolts—the processes, procedures, tools, and systems. It means getting everything to work right and getting the bugs out. The outcome of this stage can be either adopting the change or aborting it. All too often, companies are shortsighted and prematurely declare victory at this phase.

The adoption stage is the point where organizations begin to examine the long-term implications of the change. Again, the organization is faced with a choice: Either terminate the change or make it part of the standard operating procedures.

Next, the change becomes integral to the organization. It becomes institutionalized. The very nature and fabric of the organizational structure is now altered to support and nourish this new way of working, thinking, and being.

But, this still is not enough to secure the results desired from the change. People can act for reasons and motives that are not in the best long-term interests of the organization. So, the final stage represents internalization, the point where the change becomes not only integral to the organization, but also to the individual, to each person.

In your e-learning implementation, it's critical to plan for these three phases in the commitment process: preparation, acceptance, and commitment. The initial communications you deliver through newsletters, briefings, posters, and emails are all part of preparing the learners, management, and organization as a whole. Through a comprehensive change communication program, they will be able to gain an understanding of the scope of your e-learning program, what it really offers them and, based on that, you will secure their acceptance. This sets the stage for developing true individual and organizational commitment.

The trap is letting yourself focus too heavily on the installation of your e-learning—the nuts and bolts—and then declaring success. Although technically the e-learning will work, you may still fall far short of your real goals, impacting the performance of individual learners and the organization as a whole. It's only through finding ways to truly institutionalize e-learning in your organization, to make it integral to the fabric of everyday work life, that you will be able to reach these goals. And, even then, it will take each learner, each manager, each trainer, and each employee to internalize e-learning in such a way that it becomes truly second nature.

Framework for Making Organizational Change

So, you might ask, haven't people been down this road before? Organizational change is not new. Just in the past decade restructuring, restrategizing, reorganizing, reengineering, downsizing, upsizing, rightsizing, total quality, Six Sigma, and cultural renewal have swept across the corporate landscape.

According to John Kotter (1996), two conditions are necessary for successful organizational change. First, the change must be associated with a process that creates power and motivation sufficient enough to overwhelm all the counterchange forces in an organization. And second, high-quality leadership—not just management—is required. Kotter offers a useful and compelling eight-stage framework for change:

1. *Establish a sense of urgency:* Urgency trumps complacency. To be successful, a majority of the employees, 75 percent of management overall, and virtually all of the top executives must believe the change is absolutely essential.
2. *Create a guiding coalition:* Assemble a team that can direct, drive, and guide the change effort. It is a rare situation indeed that one person alone can bring about lasting organizational change. Change is truly a team sport. Getting the right team together that balances power, expertise, credibility, and leadership is, therefore, critical to success.
3. *Develop a vision and strategy:* Although vision has lost its luster over the past few years, it remains a powerful tool for change. A good vision motivates and inspires while providing a picture of what the future will look like. It breaks through resistance. A good vision clarifies the direction of the change, motivates people to take action, and serves as a focal point for all of the decisions, actions, and work that must be coordinated. Strategy

is then necessary to provide both logic and an initial level of detail to show that the vision is indeed achievable.

4. *Communicate the change vision:* The power of the vision is unleashed when most people get it. Therefore, simplicity is the key. "The time and energy required for effective vision communication are directly related to the clarity and simplicity of the message" (Kotter, 1996).

5. *Empower broad-based action:* Major change requires many people to help. People won't help, though, unless they feel their efforts make a difference. Four obstacles—structures, skills, systems, and supervisors—must be removed to allow empowerment to take root.

6. *Generate short-term wins:* Change can take time. Often the most important components can be subtle. People tend to be impatient. Only true zealots are willing to stay the course no matter what. Others need evidence or data or encouragement.

7. *Consolidate gains and produce more change:* The old way of doing things is a powerful force pulling against change. Therefore, it is important to push ahead to make more change happen. Keys to success at this stage include additional people being brought into the process; senior management maintaining the sense of urgency and clarity of vision; and management identifying and eliminating barriers.

8. *Anchor new approaches in the culture:* In Kotter's view, culture change comes last, not first. Culture is powerful. It influences everyone and everything. But, true culture change comes about as a result of new approaches, new behaviors, and new ways of thinking all sinking into the existing culture and creating a new culture. Without culture change, change will not last. The existing culture will eventually overwhelm it and return to its past state of being.

Eight Mistakes in Implementing Change
1. Allowing too much complacency
2. Failing to create a sufficiently powerful guiding coalition
3. Underestimating the power of vision
4. Undercommunicating the vision by a factor of 10 (or even 100 or 1,000)
5. Permitting obstacles to block the new vision
6. Failing to create opportunities for short-term wins
7. Neglecting to anchor changes firmly in the corporate culture
8. Declaring victory too soon

A word of caution: Kotter (1996) strongly believes that the eight steps must be done in order, that you shouldn't leave one step without finishing the work. His feeling is that each step builds upon the other. Therefore, if you take short cuts, the foundation will be weak and threaten to collapse the whole change effort. Or, you will spend more time going back and redoing steps, wasting time and energy.

Implementing e-learning is a significant organizational change, regardless of what purveyors of e-learning might tell you. You must, therefore, plan for it accordingly and apply an appropriate framework for managing the change at an organizational level.

Kotter's framework maps well what you will need to do to ensure the success of your e-learning implementation. Specifically, you need to

- create and communicate a meaningful business case that motivates learners, managers, and the entire organization
- pull together a well-respected and effective team to champion, plan for, and support your effort
- develop a compelling vision of what e-learning offers
- develop and implement a change communication program to reach all learners, managers, staff, and the greater organization
- recruit a wide base of change agents at all levels of your organization to help communicate your vision and remove obstacles, solve problems, and maintain enthusiasm
- figure out how to have some very quick successes that show clearly the benefits of e-learning: a minicourse, a module, or an online job aid
- ensure that you build on your early successes in a planned-for and coordinated fashion
- look for ways to make e-learning an integral part of your organizational culture rather than another option.

Getting Everyone on Board

So many stakeholders, so little time. With whom should you start? Fortunately, you only need to begin with a few, but it's critical to choose the right few.

Everett M. Rogers (1995) laid the groundwork in this area. He determined that people tend to fall into six distinct categories when confronted with a new innovation or change: innovators, early adopters, early majority, late majority, late adopters, and diehards (figure 2-5).

For implementing your e-learning project, you must focus on the innovators and early adopters. Innovators are those who are first to sign onto anything new, the first to try a new way of doing something. They are the risk takers and adventurers who can cope with high uncertainty. Oftentimes their peers do not know what to make of them. Early adopters tend to be the opinion leaders in an organization. They adopt new ideas early but carefully. They are internally focused and tend to be respected because of their decisions.

If you can get the innovators and a few early adopters on board with the changes required to implement e-learning, the others will follow and the

---

Figure 2-5. How people adopt change (based on the work of E.M. Rogers).

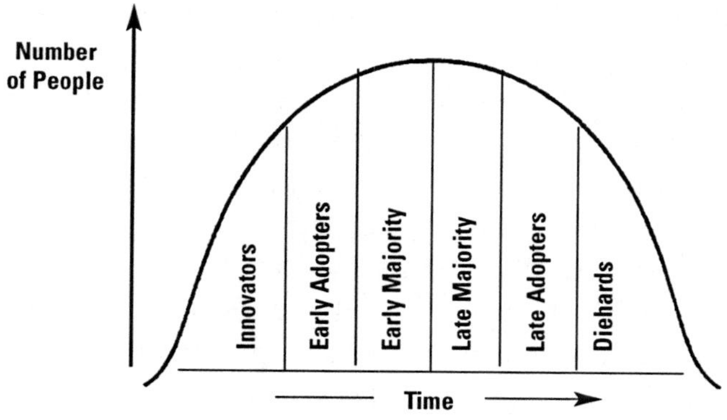

Number of People

Innovators | Early Adopters | Early Majority | Late Majority | Late Adopters | Diehards

Time →

Source: Reprinted with permission from Jaffe, D., and C. Scott. (1995). *Managing Change at Work: Leading People Through Organizational Transitions* (revised edition). Menlo Park, CA: Crisp Publications.

changes will become imbedded in the organization. Then, it's only a matter of time and numbers before the change process becomes unstoppable (figure 2-6).

If you doubt this precept, remember back to when you bought your first computer or cell phone or CD player. How many of your friends or colleagues had one already? How soon after you got yours did it seem like everyone had one? It's like the domino effect; one day only a few innovators had one, and the next day, everyone had one. And, now, no one can imagine life without one.

Figure 2-6. Building momentum for organizational change.

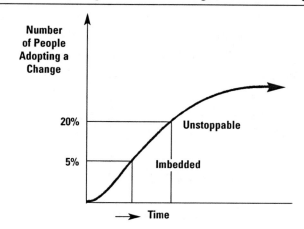

Number of People Adopting a Change

20% — Unstoppable

5% — Imbedded

Time →

Reprinted with permission from Jaffe, D., and C. Scott. (1995). *Managing Change at Work: Leading People Through Organizational Transitions* (revised edition). Menlo Park, CA: Crisp Publications.

FUNDAMENTALS OF CONSUMER MARKETING

Does the word *marketing* give you good vibes or a bad taste in your mouth? Do you think of advertising, public relations, brand management, product positioning, price optimization, segmentation, customer satisfaction, and other marketing concepts? Or do you think of snake oil salesmen, artificially inflated demand, and P.T. Barnum's "sucker born every minute"?

Marketing is the foundation of capitalist economies. Its function is to attract and keep customers. The term *marketing* as used in this book does not refer to what the folks in the marketing department do. The copywriters and flacks that give marketing its bad reputation are working on a minor subset of the discipline of marketing. As David Packard (1989) says, "Marketing is far too important to leave to the marketing department." Think of it as a never-ending process that builds mutually satisfying long-term relationships with customers by satisfying their psychological and physical needs.

Why Now?

Training department managers, e-learning administrators, human resources directors, and instructors have done without marketing for years. Why start marketing corporate learning now?

For at least a decade, training directors have mouthed the words that learning is a process, not an event. Yet they've treated it like a series of events. Courses begin and end. Drop-out rates are measured course-by-course. Big chunks of instruction (virtual or real) are typically seen to be more important than small chunks, whose just-in-time nature may make them more valuable to the learner.

E-learning is an infrastructure. It's more like going to college than taking a class. Check out the promotional material at a college Website. The site will display smiling students, photographs of the campus, and some sports activity. The words describe the school as a challenging but enjoyable place whose graduates achieve fame and fortune. The colleges know that they've got to sell the whole package, not individual courses. So do you.

Individual courses don't justify market analysis and campaigns. A major e-learning effort does because:

- E-learning is an ongoing process, not an event.
- Large investments are at stake.
- Achieving results is no longer optional.
- Many people do not understand what e-learning is.
- Skeptics are critical of its effectiveness.
- Many people don't think it's for them.

The Marketing Process

Most marketers follow a process that begins with market research, that is, scoping out what customers want, how the marketplace is structured, barriers to entry, competitive climate, demographics, and trends. Armed with this information, they craft a marketing strategy, analyzing how they intend to serve different segments of the market and where they will position their product vis-à-vis the alternatives. They plan their tactics. Campaigns kick off; plans are translated into action. Results are monitored closely, leading to revisions to the plan, renegotiating target objectives, and making midcourse corrections. If these steps seem familiar, it is because they parallel the process of instructional design (table 2-1).

The steps of both the marketing process and instructional systems design (ISD) are idealized. The real world is much messier. It's not as if you complete one step in either marketing or ISD, close it up, and go on to the next. There's constant interplay between the steps.

Note that what marketers call "developing the marketing mix" is very similar to what instructional designers refer to as "developing blended learning." In the design stage, the marketer's segmentation is parallel to the trainer's prioritization of learner populations. For example, trainers are positioning courses when they label a fundamental course as an executive seminar.

The next step is to create a comprehensive marketing plan for your e-learning. You don't have to write an elaborate marketing plan. After all, you're not a marketing executive at a major consumer products company. It's more important in the case of e-learning to apply appropriate marketing concepts than it is to spend time creating fancy plans.

The Four *P*s

The field of marketing has traditionally relied upon four basic tenets, the so-called "four *P*s." As Silicon Valley marketing legend Regis McKenna (2002)

Table 2-1. Parallels between marketing and instructional systems design.

Marketing	Instructional Systems Design
Market research	Needs analysis
Segment and position	Design
Develop marketing mix	Develop program
Implement	Implement
Respond to feedback	Evaluate

points out: "The Four *Ps*—product, pricing, place, and promotion—were introduced in the 1950s and popularized in business schools over the next forty years, reducing marketing to a generic set of theoretical principles that focused more on managing marketing's organizational and functional activities rather than on serving or satisfying customers." Marketing pros are starting to deemphasize the *Ps* in favor of a *B:* branding.

Branding

Technically, a brand is the "combination of symbols, words, or designs that differentiate one company's product from another company's product" (Clemente, 1992). But what do brand managers really do? Astute marketers know that perception is more important than reality when appealing to customers. Brands guide perceptions. Consider the implications of the following:

- *Brand association:* Do you say "Xerox" to mean photocopy or "Kleenex" to mean paper tissue?
- *Brand equity:* This term refers to the value of the promise made to customers and shareholders. The market value of Coca-Cola is $115 billion. More than $100 billion of that figure is the intangible value of Coke's brand.
- *Brand extension:* Tabasco Green Sauce, Garlic Tabasco Sauce, Tabasco t-shirts, and Tabasco neckties: These spin-off products take advantage of the halo effect of the basic Tabasco brand.
- *Brand image:* Volvo is safe. Rolls Royce is luxury. Porsche is sexy. Hummer is macho.
- *Brand loyalty:* Year after year, people buy Crest toothpaste, Sony electronics, and Honda automobiles.
- *Brand name:* Allegheny Airlines changed its name to U.S. Air when market testing showed that travelers preferred the latter. Volkswagen transformed its Rabbit model into the Golf to boost sales in Australia when marketing executives realized that rabbits are considered agricultural pests in Australia.

Why is branding important in e-learning? It's what brings new learners to your door. It's what keeps them coming back. Hayes Roth (2001), director of marketing for the branding strategy firm Landor Associates, says:

> "Branding, in effect, helps answer the customer question: 'Why should I do business with you?' From the moment a customer holds your brochure, walks into your store, looks at your

Website or holds your product, he or she begins to form an opinion about your brand and its value. Is it reliable? Is it effective? Is it up to date? Is it innovative? Is it better than the others? Is it worth the price? In a world where customers have less and less time to consider options, branding helps them make a decision that often occurs in a split second."

Consequently, branding is not about aesthetics. It's about effectively communicating your e-learning program's value and difference to create preference and generate purchases.

Eliminate Commodities

Marketers use brands to create value for their customers and stockholders. Without branding, a product is a commodity—a low-margin item that competes on price alone. Marketers "convert" commodities into valuable products.

Take salt. It's NaCl, sodium chloride. Salt is one of the most abundant chemicals on this planet and can be harvested from any ocean. Salt is salt, right? Well, no. People trust the Morton brand. "When it rains it pours." With its recognizable blue canister with a picture of a little girl holding an umbrella, it sells for 50 percent more than the other brands of table salt sharing the same shelf.

How about water? Two parts hydrogen and one part oxygen. Water is so commonplace that it falls out of the sky. It's everywhere. It covers more than half the earth. Isn't water a commodity? Hardly. Designer waters cost more than $1 a bottle. The Evian Brumisateur is a mist sprayer that contains melted snow water from the Alps, which sells for more than $1 an ounce.

Build Relationships

What you've just read is still the heart of every master's program in marketing. Little has changed in the past 25 years or so; it's all still valid. In fact, all that's new is that the goal is no longer short-term sales. The goal is relationships—long-term customer relationships. Acquiring new customers is expensive. Once you open a relationship with them, it only makes sense to sell to them again. Repeat customers are lucrative. This is why credit card companies and magazine publishers will give you a great deal to sign up with them. It's worth a few hundred dollars to them to initiate a relationship that may be worth thousands over the next decade.

You need to do the same with e-learning. You want to brand your e-learning so that your customers keep coming back for more! For example, perhaps eliminating busywork is one of the attributes you want associated with your brand.

You might structure your e-learning so learners never need enter the same information twice. You could personalize the options offered to learners, graying out subjects they have already mastered. You might provide announcements of new developments in the subject areas they have recently tackled.

Blurring the Line

Before the rise of relationships between buyer and seller, suppliers sold products (tangible things) and services (things that are simultaneously consumed and delivered). Buyers bought what sellers sold. Buyers might get a little extra on this transaction and a little less on the next.

Now the line between products and services has begun to fade. Buyers sell and sellers buy. Customers don't deal with employees from one supplier; they deal with members of the vendor's ecosystem. "No longer is there a clear line between structure and process, owning and using, knowing and learning, real and virtual" (Davis & Meyer, 1998). Rather, "offers" replace traditional products and services.

Why offers? Offers provide you the opportunity to co-develop the learning experience with the learner. Bear in mind that the learning experience doesn't exist until both you and your customer co-create it. In the bad old days when training was considered a product, many organizations thought conducting a standard workshop or throwing a CD over the cubicle wall was sufficient. Today, the concept of the e-learning offer recognizes that successful learning involves give and take. E-learning provides resources; learners take what's appropriate to their needs.

The Cluetrain Arrives

Marketing is an attitude, a process, and a set of tools. As McKenna (1991) says, "Marketing must find a way to integrate the customer into the company—to create and sustain a relationship. It's not a function—it's a way of doing business."

This integration of customers represents a fundamental shift. Customers have the power, the tools, and the moxie to deal directly with corporations. After years being mere consumers, customers are now in control, and markets have become conversations. Perhaps the *Cluetrain Manifesto* (Locke et al., 2001) says it best:

> "What's happening to the market is precisely what should—and will—happen to marketing. Marketing needs to become a craft. Recall that craftworkers listen to the material they're forming,

shaping the pot to the feel of the clay, designing the house to fit with and even reveal the landscape. The stuff of marketing is the market itself. Marketing can't become a craft until it can hear the new—the old—sound of its markets. By listening, marketing will re-learn how to talk."

That's why in this book, marketing means focusing on your customers—your learners—to the exclusion of all else. That's how good organizations become great. It's not schlock; it's purity of purpose. It's not tricks; it's honest conversation. Marketing is about developing and keeping long-term, profitable relationships with customers. That's how you implement successful e-learning and keep them coming back for more.

YOUR TURN

Implementing e-learning requires a two-pronged approach: change management and effective marketing. To help you think in these terms, tackle worksheets 2-1 and 2-2.

Worksheet 2-1. A change for the better.

Think of three examples of changes in your job that you felt were positive.

1. _____

2. _____

3. _____

Why do you think these changes were good? What role did change management have in determining the positive aspects of these changes?

(continued on page 28)

Worksheet 2-1. A change for the better (continued).

What might your learners welcome about e-learning? Jot down three possibilities here:

1. _____

2. _____

3. _____

What might your learners dread about e-learning? Jot down three possibilities here:

1. _____

2. _____

3. _____

Worksheet 2-2. Start on your marketing plan.

1. How do you think marketing e-learning is different from marketing other products or services?

2. What will be the main barriers to developing a marketing approach for your e-learning? Check all that apply:

☐ Carrying out market research

☐ Developing an e-learning brand

☐ Changing the view that e-learning is a commodity

☐ Establishing long-term learner/customer relationships

☐ Buying into the concept of e-learning as an offer, not a product or service

3

Preparing for Successful Implementation

Implementing e-learning is not just about getting people to actually use the e-learning. It is also about how to ensure that people internalize e-learning over the long term, and that depends on whether they believe in the value and purpose of e-learning and act accordingly over time. An effective implementation program must move people from being able to understand the reasons why e-learning is something they *should* use to being *ready, willing, and able* to embrace the next wave of e-learning (figure 3-1).

In this chapter you will learn about some key concepts, practices, and tactics to help you construct a solid foundation for the successful implementation of your e-learning.

Figure 3-1. Success happens when people are ready, willing, and able.

ORGANIZATIONS ARE SYSTEMS

Organizations are dynamic systems in which the change in one element necessitates changes in all the others. Many models have been developed to represent this fact graphically; after all, a picture is worth a thousand words.

The 7-*S* model was developed by Tom Peters and Robert Waterman when they were at the management consulting firm McKinsey & Company (figure 3-2).

The model includes three hard *S*s—strategy, structure, and systems—and four soft *S*s—style (culture), staff, skills, and shared values. The hard *S*s are easy to see and understand. They can be found in strategy documents, corporate plans, and organizational charts. The soft *S*s are more difficult to identify and describe because they represent the capabilities, values, and elements of corporate culture that are constantly changing and evolving. Moreover, because people in the organization determine them, soft *S*s are much more difficult to influence and predict.

Another way to look at your organization is by using a business system diamond model and its later variants. This model became popular during the reengineering revolution of the late 1990s (figure 3-3), championed by Michael Hammer and James Champy. In this model, no distinction is made between hard and soft variables.

What this models shows is that when a business process such as e-learning changes, then the technology and information systems that enable it also must

Figure 3-2. The McKinsey 7-*S* model.

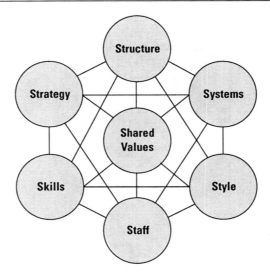

Source: Reprinted with permission from McKinsey & Company.

Figure 3-3. The business diamond model.

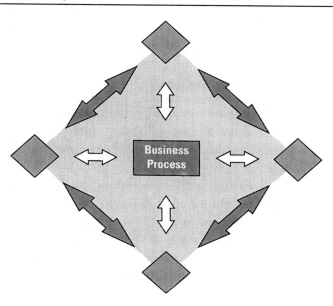

change. This change, in turn, affects the way jobs and the organization are structured, which then affect the way management and management systems are designed. The adapted management and management systems will then shape the values and beliefs of the employees and the culture of the organization.

It is interesting to note, however, the 1994 "State of Reengineering" report by CSC Index stated that 50 percent of the companies that participated in the study reported the most difficult part of reengineering was dealing with the fear and anxiety in their organizations.

THE SYSTEMS APPROACH FOR IMPLEMENTING E-LEARNING

The technological impacts are easy. Learners may need sound cards and headphones that are not currently part of the standard, approved configuration. But, if learners are able to register and access learning activities directly online, how does that change the role of the front-line manager who now reviews and approves all requests? And, if learners can now learn at their desks, how does that affect the organizational values that encourage walk-in, open door or "over-the-cubicle" interactions? Build a foundation for success by answering questions like these.

CULTURE ALWAYS WINS

On the positive side, you are not beginning with a cultural "blank slate." Your organization has a well-defined culture already. Its attributes stare you in the face each and every day. For example, it is difficult to imagine a longtime employee of Southwest Airlines, Oracle, WalMart, or Club Med easily changing cultures. The shared patterns and attitudes—often unspoken—that permeate these organizations belong solely to these organizations.

Assessing Your Organization's Culture

Your organization has its own culture, and it is important to use this culture to your advantage. If the structure of your e-learning does not fit the corporate culture, it will probably fail. One way to get a handle on your corporation's culture is to look at its artifacts.

Imagine that you are visiting your company offices for the first time. What stands out? Is senior management all up on the top floor? Do managers have offices and workers cubicles? What hangs on the walls, original art or motivation posters or nothing at all? Is headquarters in a spiffy glass skyscraper or a trendy loft or a Quonset hut? Is the parking lot filled with sport-utility vehicles or Honda Accords or Porsches? Do employees wear suits or "corporate casual" clothing or corporate uniforms? Another way to unveil the culture of your organization is to ask a variety of questions and then search for patterns and meaning among the answers. Try some of these:

- What's most important here?
- How does a person get ahead here?
- Name five words that sum this place up.
- What's the attitude toward making mistakes?
- Does what employees do on their own time matter?
- Are most employees enthusiastic about the company or critical of it?
- Are people proud to work here?
- What drives staff turnover?
- Do people collaborate or are they loners?
- Do front-line people make decisions or follow orders?
- Does everyone know his or her role in fulfilling the corporate vision?

Distinct Features of Your Corporate Culture

If your organization operates in more than one country, you will want to assess differences in local cultures that affect your programs. Geert Hofstede, a psychologist at IBM, studied the influence of cultural values on workplace values in 40 countries. By analyzing more than 100,000 individuals between 1967 and 1973, he isolated five dimensions to aid in understanding cultural differences between regions and countries. His work is now the foundation for cross-cultural value studies worldwide. The five dimensions are:

Equality ←——————→ Inequality
Individualism ←——————→ Collectivism
Masculine ←——————→ Gender equality
Risk-averse ←——————→ Pro-change
Long-term ←——————→ In the moment

If all this feels like you are trying to be a cultural anthropologist, you are half right. You, in fact, do need to be somewhat of an anthropologist to be successful in this phase. Uncovering these attributes enables you to then design and carry out an implementation strategy that is truly tailored for your organization.

READY, SET, GO!

You have probably already conducted some type of general e-learning readiness assessment, but now you should conduct a readiness assessment specifically for e-learning implementation. The purpose is not to determine if or when, but rather how e-learning will be implemented. As you can imagine, there are as many models as opinions about what areas need to be assessed. The sections that follow address some of the models' common themes.

Culture

Culture readiness refers to the necessary values, attitudes, and behaviors surrounding your e-learning process. The work you have already completed above will get you started. In this assessment you need to focus on how learning works in the culture of your organization.

Here are the types of questions you need to be asking:

- What is your organization's definition of learning, and how does it view the role of learning?
- Who is responsible for employee development and learning—the manager, the organization, or the employee?
- How is learning currently managed and organized?
- What does the organization measure and value (attendance, certification, test scores, work performance, and so forth)?
- Does the organization value learning outside the classroom?
- What have been your organization's prior experiences with technology-delivered or -enabled learning (computer-based training, DVDs)?

Transitioning from instructor-led training to e-learning is usually a pretty big cultural shift associated with many divergent forces. You are trying to change years—if not decades—of familiar, instructor-led training that learners have relied upon not only in the organization, but also in the educational system they were part of for most of their growing-up years. People know how to do it. Trainers know how to present it. Your organization knows how to manage it.

Technology

Technological readiness addresses the physical (hardware, infrastructure, information technology support) elements necessary for your e-learning to work. It's often the lack of attention to technical details that transforms a good experience into a bad one. When going through change, people are under stress and have a very low tolerance for things that don't work. What doesn't work reinforces resistance ("I knew this wouldn't work!"). Little things become big barriers.

You must gather information so that you can answer questions like these:

- What is your current standard PC configuration?
- Will it support your e-learning programs (large audio and video files, access to the Internet)?
- Do all the intended audience members for your e-learning programs have PC access? If not, how will they get it?
- How will learners log on?
- What about printing?
- How about access from home?

You must drill down to a fine level of detail; you have to consider every scenario.

Capability

The term *capability* refers to the skills, knowledge, and abilities required in your organization to ensure the success of your implementation. The questions you are seeking answers to include these:

- Who will provide technical support for your e-learners?
- Who will provide subject matter expertise?
- Who will manage your suppliers and vendors?
- Where will you find your internal change agents?
- Who will manage the overall change implementation process?
- Who will oversee the communications process?

Organization

Organizational readiness refers to the governance structures needed to support your e-learning. Your questions should include these:

- Which group has the overall responsibility for e-learning?
- Who is responsible for managing suppliers?
- Who is responsible for standards, tools, and technologies?
- Who determines effectiveness and business impact?
- Who is to equip trainers with the skills they need?

LEADERS COME IN ALL SHAPES AND SIZES

"Leadership defines what the future should look like, aligns people with that vision, and inspires them to make it happen despite the obstacles" (Kotter, 1996). Identifying, harnessing, and supporting the power of leadership are critical success factors for your e-learning implementation.

Who Are the Leaders?

Leaders come in all sizes and shapes, from all parts of your organization. Some have big titles and large offices. Others may be sitting next to you in a cubicle. Leadership is, above all, a set of recognizable behaviors that can be seen and heard by anyone in your organization. By this definition, leadership is not reserved exclusively for persons "in positions of authority." Rather, leadership can be exercised by anyone, at any time, under circumstances requiring them to behave in leader-like ways. Leaders are distinguished by their ability to communicate and motivate and their willingness to participate. Leaders are antidotes to the natural resistance and fear that crop up when an organization is faced with a change. Leaders can act as catalysts for your e-learning implementation and the changes that need to take place.

You need to identify the important leaders who have senior management roles and titles in key business units, information technology (IT), and training/human resources.

> ### Be Absolutely, Positively Sure That It Works
>
> Based on the readiness assessment, test all the technology. Nothing will undermine your implementation faster than the simple stuff—learners who can't log-on, add-ons that don't work, missing sound and video cards, lack of headphones and/or microphones, firewall issues that go unresolved, incompatible software, slow connections, confusing user interface, "file not found," clumsy navigation, 404 errors, poor response time, and the "blue screen of death." Remember as well that some learners may be several operating systems behind and connecting to the Net with a standard telephone line in a developing nation.
>
> Everyone has a limit for this sort of thing. The seemingly little stuff takes on much large proportion in the midst of a change such as this.

In addition, you need to identify key influencers in each of these areas. These are the individuals other people listen to even though—and maybe because—they don't have formal roles and titles. And, you also need to identify the informal leaders who are willing to take on the role of internal change agents.

A Tale of Two Companies

There is definitely more than one way to manage the change associated with an e-learning implementation. Which one you choose—and which one is best for your organization—will become evident as you review the findings from your readiness assessment. Here is how Procter and Gamble (P&G) and The Limited created their own implementation strategies.

At P&G, one key aspect of e-learning implementation has been to substitute e-learning for instructor-led courses (ILT). At times, the "carrot approach" is used to get people to switch by offering e-learning to departments free of charge. At other times ILT programs were cancelled to force learners to try e-learning. As director of P&G's corporate learning center at the time, Larry Green is quoted as saying, "To change the culture, you've got to put some pressure on. You can't just wait for the culture to be ready." The results? In a 10-month period, P&G went from a curriculum mix of 5 percent e-learning to 63 percent. The stated goal is to increase this percentage even more and end up with 90 percent of all learning e-enabled in some way.

At The Limited, coexistence is a dominant theme. ILT and e-learning offerings cover the same content. Associates can choose which they prefer. Over time, e-learning acceptance and usage has gone up, but ILT remains a strong part of the overall learning strategy. Based on The Limited's culture and workforce, the preferred e-learning change strategy is one of blending and choices rather than replacement.

Assessing Leadership Readiness

Your assessment must look at the formal and informal structures that can ensure not only initial acceptance but also provide ongoing support. Without leadership at all levels and from all levels, acceptance of your e-learning will be slow, if it comes at all. And, without acceptance, your e-learning initiative will have a very short shelf life.

The readiness assessment process can range from the informal (interviews) to the formal (surveys and questionnaires). The important thing is to get a broad representation in your data collection, covering all the main target audiences and stakeholders.

Leadership Is the Key

From this perspective of leadership, two basic conditions must be met for you to be successful:

1. Leadership must be embodied in many individuals, some with the mantle of authority, some not.
2. These individuals must behave like leaders in concert with one another.

Organizations like Intel, IBM, ANZ, and Commonwealth Bank have identified a wide variety of leaders, ranging from top managers to direct supervisors to evangelists, for their e-learning implementations. They use phrases like "leadership is critical," "go to the top first," "driven by line managers," "executive sponsorship is key," and "buy-in from business leaders" when describing the role of leadership in their successful implementations.

Leadership From the Top

Your e-learning implementation needs a sponsor or two. Sponsors are responsible for championing the case for change, visibly representing the change, and reassuring learners. Depending on your organization, you may need one sponsor to secure senior support at the highest levels while another sponsor drives the change down into the organization.

Characteristics of effective sponsors include

- commitment to the implementation
- great communication skills
- understanding of the change process
- high integrity and honesty
- sensitivity to both politics and people
- respect from throughout the organization
- tolerance for risk
- thick skin.

Leadership From Within

Other leaders often go unrecognized and unappreciated. They do not wear the formal mantle of authority. Nonetheless, they drive change from within. In effect they are the ones who sell the change to the organization. They are called change agents and are critical to the implementation and acceptance of change within your organization. And, to be successful with your e-learning implementation, you will need as many of these change agents as you can find and support.

E-Learning Leadership

Beth Thomas, director of the LTS Learning Center at The Limited, early on secured the support and sponsorship of the chief operating officer. She prepared a targeted presentation for him in his language—the language of business and money. Once he was sold on her plan, he championed the plan at the senior leadership level. He was her sponsor to manage "up" and to sponsor her e-learning programs within the organization. Beth identified other senior business leaders at the business-unit level. They are closest to the action—where the need is and where the results are felt. This dual approach enabled her to keep her ongoing and future e-learning initiatives in alignment with the organization.

Companies as diverse as Novartis and Charter Communications have formed e-learning task forces to help prepare their organizations for e-learning. Membership includes senior managers representing all the key departments and functions. They meet regularly with the guidance of an outside consultant. They are a visible sign of leadership and commitment.

Change agents secure initial acceptance and buy-in for your e-learning initiative and then facilitate the change process necessary for full implementation. They may be self-appointed (from the innovators) or selected (from the early adopters) for their technical expertise, skill sets, or organizational influence. Change agents come from all levels within the organization and all parts of the organization. They must be excellent communicators and great at selling people on new ideas. They ask tough questions of those in power and actively influence implementation planning, while being diplomatic. Finally, they must be committed to the change and able to handle its by-products: criticism and resistance. Specifically, change agents

- serve as advance communicators who clarify expectations and deal with technological fears
- act as facilitators for change events
- provide information regarding the project
- act as subject matter experts
- provide feedback for midcourse corrections by collecting data via questionnaires, interviews, and focus groups.

Executive Support Is Paramount

"Nothing is more important than executive support," says Aspect Communication's Kara Underwood. "You must align your activities to the executives' points of pain. You must measure success with their metrics." To succeed, organizational learning must be strategic. Managers of training must make it clear that they don't think of their jobs as merely creating training. Rather, their job is to support the strategic direction of the firm. It's also important to provide feedback from constituents, according to Underwood. She reviews results and anecdotes in monthly one-on-one sessions with senior sales staff and others.

Laura Keziah, vice president of operations and technology training at Compass Bank, says she recognized early that senior management did not have a clear picture of e-learning and what it could do to improve performance. She set 15-minute appointments with seven senior executives. At the beginning of each one-to-one meeting, she would put her watch on the table and state that because she only had 15 minutes, she wanted to make every second count and would ask two leading questions:

1. Do you understand how e-learning can help the bank meet its objectives?
2. Which performance issues that e-learning might address keep you up at night?

The interviews unearthed questions the execs had been hesitant to ask in an open forum. What is e-learning? What is the difference between e-learning and computer-based training? Five of the seven execs extended the 15-minute sessions to an hour.

With an understanding of the basics of the e-learning platform, the executives could ask informed questions about the bank's investments in learning. The issue was no longer whether the bank would use e-learning, but how.

Due to the highly visible roles change agents play, they should be selected based on the following personal attributes and characteristics:

- good interpersonal communication skills
- influential, credible, and respected in regions
- capable of self-management
- able to coordinate multiple logistics
- willing to speak publicly
- tolerant of ambiguity
- able to balance multiple tasks and priorities
- willing to assume a leadership role
- willing to work behind the scene
- knowledgeable about operations.

At The Limited, pilot teams for e-learning implementations are made up of business representatives from all levels in the target audience plus the IT department. This group reviews and tests e-learning programs before they go live. Moreover, these teams serve an important role once the implementation begins as internal change agents. During the launch, the members of this group become superusers and its most ardent evangelists.

Losing Faith in E-Learning

A large consulting firm was hired to create e-learning to teach the principles of free cash flow to 5,000 managers. Several hundred thousand dollars later, the consulting firm handed off an e-learning package showing the benefits of free cash flow. People who participated in the pilot loved the program and came away feeling that they could put it to work. Nevertheless, the e-learning was an abysmal failure. Of the 5,000 managers, only 150 showed up to explore the e-learning and significantly fewer completed it.

What went wrong? Management was unwilling to endorse the program and champion its use. Despite the consultant's advice, they refused to hold learners accountable or to provide incentives for participation. Senior management was also not interested in dismantling the corporate silos that were ingrained in the organization's culture.

On Your Way to Success

In this chapter you have seen that because organizations are systems, you need to be thinking about more than just how your e-learning functionally works. You need to be planning ways to support the necessary changes in all aspects of your organization. You have also seen how the culture and leadership are critical success factors in your e-learning implementation. "Culture always wins." Remember this phrase, internalize it, and act as if it is your mantra. And, finally, find and nourish the leaders who will come from all levels and areas of your organization for they are key to making this change to e-learning a success.

YOUR TURN

Because culture and leadership have been identified as two key factors, take a few minutes to jumpstart your thinking by jotting down your answers to the questions posed in worksheet 3-1.

Worksheet 3-1. Assess your organization's culture.

1. Identify one key issue you anticipate you will face in each of the "bases" of the diamond illustration noted in figure 3-3.

2. What artifacts typify your organization's culture?

3. What are the distinct features of your corporate culture?

4. What differences in regional cultures need to be accommodated in your delivery of e-learning?

5. What strategy will work best in your culture and why?

6. Who are your likely leaders and why?

7. Who are your likely change agents and why?

8. List all the technical issues that need to be considered.

4

Really Communicate

Communication is the starting point for engaging your people and gaining their commitment to the change to e-learning. The importance and power of communication during change efforts cannot be underestimated. First, it is the way the sponsors deliver the vision and strategy to the organization. Second, it is the means to develop understanding of the change and the progress of the change process. Third, it is the mechanism for sending and receiving two-way communication and enabling dialogue between all the stakeholders.

It is essential to communicate in a timely manner during a change effort, to communicate often throughout its duration, and to use a variety of vehicles to communicate. The best communication approach informs, educates, engages, motivates, mobilizes, creates support and agreement, and generates commitment.

VISION

A vision statement is a picture of what you want the future to look like. It is something that will require significant change and progress to attain—a stretch. A vision becomes real for people through communication and conversation, which offer people the opportunity to gain awareness of what is changing and to actively engage in planning the change. By talking through the "What if," the "I'm not sure," the "Let's add this," the "Tell me more," the "What do I need to do?" people become comfortable with the new idea. They start to imagine what their lives would be like living the vision. They start to ask questions, to get excited, to add their own ideas, to make the vision their own. Finally, they begin to develop commitment to make the vision work for themselves and the organization.

A vision statement for an e-learning implementation might be something like one of the following:

- On-time performance 24/7/365
- R^4: The Right learning at the Right place at the Right time in the Right amount
- Learning anytime, anywhere
- Performance at your fingertips.

MISSION

A mission statement is an extension of the vision statement. Once you decide what you want the future to look like, in other words, the vision statement, you need to describe why you want it to be that way. The mission statement, however, does more than describe. It reflects and examines the project's purpose, and it expresses its sense of value. Perhaps most important, it inspires us to stand out, and it guides our leaders. In addition, the process of creating the mission provides an opportunity to include more players in the ownership of and commitment to the project.

Together the vision and mission statements provide meaning and motivation to inspire and guide exceptional performance. In addition, the process of creating these statements is a continuing expansion of ownership and commitment to the project.

For an e-learning implementation the mission statement might read thus: "Our mission is to create and implement an e-learning environment that leverages technology to enable, extend, and enhance learning for all employees, customers, and suppliers."

PROJECT IDENTITY

Every successful e-learning implementation includes the creation and communication of a strong project identity, based on the vision and mission. The identity becomes the theme that is used in all communications, educational components, and training modules. The elements of a project identity are a name, icon, tagline, and color scheme. Used in combination, these elements create consistency and coherence that produce and build recognition, familiarity, understanding, and alignment.

An icon is a graphic symbol that can effectively characterize an organization, a project, or a product. Taglines are two- or three-word phrases that define and describe so as to add meaning and inject a sense of spirit. Together, they function as a clearly defined unit that speaks for the project. For example, P&G used the tagline, "The Right Learning, Right Now" with a graphic icon made from the words *rapid* and *learn*. Another example comes from Aspect Communications (figure 4-1). The owl connotes wisdom but its smile is friendly and welcoming. The professionally drawn cartoon sets expectations that the learning to follow will also be thoughtfully crafted. The mortarboard suggests that learning has its rewards.

CHANGE COMMUNICATION PLAN

You may be saying, "Been there, done that. No one listens." True enough. But, the failure is not a result of the vision or the mission—or the implementation itself. What you're experiencing is the failure of the change communication plan.

A compelling vision, a motivating mission, a cool brand, and convincing messages are meaningless unless they are communicated to the people in the organization in exciting and memorable ways. An effective change communication plan is strategic in nature although very tactical in application. It's a powerful tool for transforming your organization's priorities and the behaviors of its people. And, most important, it can serve as a catalyzing agent for the changes necessary for your e-learning implementation to be a raving success.

The change communication plan should coordinate specific activities with the general stages of your implementation plan. For example, in the early stages, your focus is on creating awareness and understanding. In the middle stages, it's on generating motivation, confidence, and involvement. And, in the final stages, the emphasis is on commitment through action and learning. An effective plan maps the messages, the activities, and the audiences to these stages.

Few people are willing to sign up for something new before they even know what it is! It's therefore unreasonable to expect any of your stakeholders to embrace your e-learning without any thought. In fact, your stakeholders will move through three distinct stages. First, they will acquire a basic awareness.

Figure 4-1. The eye-catching icon that is part of the Learning Center's identity.

Source: Reprinted with permission from the Learning Center, Aspect Communications. 2002.

Then they'll want to try it, to become engaged, to get involved. Finally, through hands-on experiences that are reinforced by timely communications, they will become committed to your e-learning (figure 4-2). As things change, this cycle will start all over again!

GUIDING PRINCIPLES

The goal of every recommended activity, educational component, consulting session, meeting, and communication is to build a community of people, at all levels of the organization, who are aware of, engaged in, and committed to the successful implementation of e-learning within your organization. Every component should be easily traced back to supporting the vision and mission.

All communications should send consistent messages across all organizational levels, across all organizational functions, and across all organizational regions. Everyone affected should receive consistent, timely information. While stressing the importance of giving consistent messages, it is important to be sensitive to regional and cultural differences in leadership style and communication delivery preferences. Plans must be purposely flexible to accommodate those differences. Keep in mind these important factors:

▪ *Keep sponsorship visible:* The highest levels of the organization's leadership and support for the implementation of the recommended programs and activities is imperative. It must be clear at all times and to all employees who is backing and supporting the project. Visible sponsorship may be spoken ("I am committed to seeing this project through to

---

Figure 4-2. The communication cycle.

- Speeches
- Memos
- Newsletters
- Magazines
- Team meetings

Awareness, *Inform*

Commitment, *Sign-up*

- Videos
- Labs and fairs
- Town meetings
- Demos
- Small group meetings

- One-on-one communication
- Team work
- Events and ceremonies

Engagement, *Involve*

completion") or, more powerfully, may be through visible actions (securing resources, including funding, people, time, space, equipment, contracts with suppliers and business partners, and so forth).

■ *Communicate a clear vision:* Given that the success of this project depends upon the cooperation and integration of work of many parties, it is imperative that leadership be of one mind to provide the glue that holds together such a massive undertaking. Gaps in leadership understanding, engagement, and commitment are very quickly noted by employees and result in waning enthusiasm and, ultimately, disappointing returns on an enormous investment.

■ *Remember that everyone is responsible for project success:* All employees, from top management on down, need to know what they are responsible for accomplishing; what authority they have to accomplish their work; how they will be held accountable for performing their work; and how their work performance will be measured and evaluated.

■ *Provide feedback mechanisms:* People naturally tend to correct themselves if they have access to "mirrors"—mechanisms that reflect back what has been accomplished and how. Regular feedback sessions, interviews, surveys, and focus groups allow for midcourse corrections that can be accomplished painlessly.

■ *Deliver honest, consistent, and credible content:* Information must be delivered by credible communicators. Messages should always be consistent with other messages, actions, and company initiatives, and they must be in tune with the organizational culture. Information should always be truthful.

DETERMINING WHAT TO COMMUNICATE

In the previous chapter, you clarified your overall mandate. With those objectives in mind, it's time to go to work on marketing.

Next, you're going to put on your market research director hat to assess your customers and prospects, the reputation of past efforts, the current situation in your company, challenges to overcome, and the greater environment outside. That's the topic of chapter 5.

In future chapters, you'll draw on your research as you morph into a marketing designer. You'll assess the payback of various segmentation schemes. You'll position your product vis-à-vis its competition. You'll paint the big picture.

You'll then think like a marketing executive as you put together the optimal combination of promotion, packaging, and product attributes to reach your objective. There is no set formula for planning; it's a creative, reflective process. What's important in one market may be trivial in another.

Throughout the whole process, you'll be keeping your finger on the pulse of all your stakeholders and your organization, ensuring that you have in place the necessary change management activities and support systems. After all, the bottom line is that your e-learning implementation is a change: change for your learners, for their managers, and for your organization as a whole.

YOUR TURN

Now it's time to stop, reflect on your situation, and apply what you've been reading. Or, if you've already begun, it's time to review what you've done and look for ways to make improvements. Either way, the elements of communication—vision, mission, project identity, and communication plan—are the foundation for a successful e-learning implementation. Use worksheet 4-1 to record each element of your situation.

Worksheet 4-1. Vision, Mission, Project Identity, and Communication Plan.

1. Draft a one-sentence vision statement for your e-learning implementation or improve the one you have.

2. Draft a mission statement for your e-learning implementation or improve the one you have.

3. Draft a tagline and icon to serve as your project identity or improve the one you have.

4. Draft the key messages, activities, and audiences for your change communication plan during preparation, during launch, and to sustain your implementation. Or, improve the change communication plan you have.

5

Analyzing the Environment of the Marketplace

Once upon a time, a brief in-house needs analysis was sufficient for launching a new training initiative. Those days are gone. In today's networked world, everything is connected. To implement e-learning successfully, you'll need to look beyond the needs of learners to executive sponsors, corporate goals, technology trends, and the future shape of your industry. This chapter is going to walk you through the process of gathering information in these areas:

- your consumers, the learners
- consumer behavior
- competitors for consumers' attention
- sponsors
- your brand image
- organizational goals
- your industry's environment
- macroeconomic environment
- trends in e-learning technology.

This chapter covers each of these areas one by one and then asks you to document your findings in a brief market research report. First, though, take a look at some best practices in research that apply to numerous areas.

RESEARCH METHODS

Market research means collecting and analyzing information about markets, organizations, and people in order to make better decisions. You must research your market to understand your learners' needs and how well you've been meeting them. Often you'll collect some new information specifically for your needs (primary data) and review information someone else has already collected (secondary data).

You can gather primary data through direct observation and surveys. You can conduct surveys on the telephone, by mail or email, or in person. Surveys are easy to conduct but often produce misleading results.

Closed-end questions (those that ask for yes or no answers) are subject to misinterpretation and may overlook important overriding factors. Open-end questions (that ask for an opinion) provide much more valuable information. Researchers like closed-end questions for the same reason teachers like true/false tests: They are simple to score.

Often you learn more by interviewing a dozen people in person than by polling hundreds of them. Advertising and market research companies sometimes conduct focus groups, which are really group interviews. Interviewing a bunch of people at once saves time and money, but whether it provides better information is questionable. Here is a case in point: One consultant was asked to review the results of focus group sessions that asked directors of training, chief learning officers, and learners about e-learning. These were full-scale sessions costing tens of thousands of dollars and moderated by professionals in conference rooms with two-way mirrors in New York, Atlanta, Chicago, and Los Angeles. At the end of the day, the e-learning consultant was forced to tell the client that the expensive exercise yielded nothing important toward the company's understanding of implementing e-learning. The sad truth is, focus groups are often poor vehicles to garner the information you need to successfully implement e-learning.

General Before Specific

There are two approaches to researching just about anything. You can go in equipped with a list of specific things you want to find out, perhaps even categorized in a formal questionnaire. Alternatively, you can wade in with a general notion of what's important to cover and let the inquiry takes its course. Start with the general inquiry face-to-face. Keep things open-ended and see what pops up. This approach keeps you from missing an important category of information solely because you didn't think of it ahead of time. After you have got your arms around what you want to know, turn to more structured inquiry.

Direct Observation

The most effective research for most in-house learning situations is direct observation and interviews. It's shocking how few chief learning officers have actually observed people learning. When they do, they quickly discover that the desktop is not the idyllic place to learn they had imagined. Most learners don't have private offices; they can't shut the door to keep out interruption. The "police line" barrier strips distributed by some companies are cute but they don't stop the telephone from ringing, nor do they keep people from dropping by to chat.

To get a true idea of people's learning environments, you need to act like a detective. Take photographs. Better still, take a video. You see things you missed when you look back at the scene the second or third time. Watch the video without the sound. Study the learner's motions. How could things be improved?

In-Person Interviews

Conduct interviews and take notes. Personal interviews with the learner and the learner's supervisor can focus on both the learning experience and the learner's motivation to learn. Inquire about what's worked in the past and what has flopped. What suggestions do they have for making things better?

You can ask questions like these:

- How have you learned to do your job? What works for you?
- What do you like about professional development at our organization?
- What would be more effective for you?
- Where do you participate in e-learning programs? At your desk? At the learning center? At home?
- What's been your experience with our new e-learning programs?
- How does training here compare with what you've experienced at other companies?
- Do our learning initiatives help you do a better job?
- Does your supervisor support your learning?

Surveys

After you have formed opinions from direct observation and face-to-face interviews, you may want to broaden your inquiry with telephone surveys and online polls. Surveys and polls are a useful way to test your hypotheses and seek advice on organizational learning. These indirect methods are often the only way to gather information from the remote corners of the enterprise. Also, your inquiries give everyone a degree of psychological ownership of what's to come.

Leave a door open for anonymously submitted information. Post and publicize a suggestion box or, more likely, its electronic equivalent.

ELEMENTS OF YOUR MARKET RESEARCH

Now you're prepared to research each of the topics introduced at the beginning of the chapter. As you form opinions in each category, jot down your thoughts in the Your Turn exercise at the end of this chapter.

Your Consumers

Who are the learners? What's in it for them? How many are there? Where? Are they technologically savvy? Do they have access to technology? Are they new hires or old hands? Are there generation gap issues? What do learners need to know? What's the impact on the bottom line?

Use the 80/20 rule. Pick the half-dozen groups of learners that could have the greatest impact on the bottom line. For each group, fill out a target consumer description that lists who the consumers are, how many there are, their location, average tenure, turnover rate, number of new hires, the consumers' learning needs, the identity of the line sponsor, and the bottom-line impact you expect from your e-learning. Figure 5-1 provides a couple of examples to help you along.

Consumer Behavior

What will it take to form a successful relationship with the consumers? Who are your prospects? What do they buy? How do they choose? Empathize with the learner. What would lead learners to embrace e-learning or to reject it?

An e-learner may not buy what you're selling because of personal fears. It's not uncommon to confront fear of failure, fear of change, fear of technology, fear of isolation, or fear of increased workload. Rebellion against a dark vision of a future where machines threaten the existence of humanity is a strong undercurrent in some people's lives. To counter the suspicion that computers will be replacing live instructors, look for opportunities to bring people back into the picture through online support, tutors, mentors, coaches, peer collaboration, and study groups.

> ### Really Bad E-Learning
>
> A colleague who had led a successful training company for 25 years was required to attend traffic school to avoid getting points on his driver's license for speeding. He was offered several alternatives, among them five hours of online instruction or a course taught by a clown who provided free pizza. "No contest," he said. "Send in the clowns." He found the thought of enduring five hours of e-learning abhorrent. "I'd rather attend a daylong course led by a mime," the traffic violator said.

Competitors

You may think that your e-learning has no competition, but you do. E-learning puts a demand on learners' time. If e-learners don't "buy" your e-learning, there are plenty of other things to occupy their time. In fact, you have competitors for learners' attention at several levels; each calls for a different competitive response.

A skeptical learner may not recognize that a deficiency in skill or knowledge is a problem. Your learner may not believe that corporate learning is the right

---

Figure 5-1. Two examples of consumer target descriptions.

Target Consumers

Group #1:   U.S. field salesforce
Number: 2,230
Location: 50% assigned to major metro offices; 50% domiciled in home office
Average Tenure: 6 years with the company.
Turnover: 12% annually.
New Hires: 275

Learning Needs:

- Product information on six launches/year
- Just-in-time precall preparation
- Convert from point sales to system sales
- Basic company services and culture intro for new hires
- Less reinventing the wheel on sales steps
- Compliance with new OSHA regulations

Line Sponsor:

Angus Sweeney, EVP Global Sales

Bottom-Line Impact Expected:

- Reduce salesforce time to productivity
- Increase deal size by 10%
- Decrease costs for OSHA training

Group #2:   Outbound telemarketing
Number: 320
Location: 120 Bahamas, 200 Bangalore
Average Tenure: 9 months with the company
Turnover: 32% annually
New hires: 120

Learning Needs:

- Product information on new products
- Customer service skills
- Blue Pumpkin automation
- Selling benefits
- Refreshers in "American" English

Line Sponsors:

Jorge Gonfrido, VP Direct Sales
Indira Singh, Director, Asia Sales Coordination

Bottom-Line Impact Expected:

- Faster ramp on new products
- More efficient call practices, less overhead time
- Shift more selling to telemarketing

Your E-Learning Environment

A major organization appoints a chief learning officer who marshals the resources to put together a rapid-response e-learning infrastructure. After ramping up, learners can tap into their personal learning portal. The e-learning system knows what they've already learned or tested out of. The system matches this profile against the competencies their job requires and dynamically assembles a personalized learning path for each learner. This self-regulating system builds intellectual capital and creates competitive advantage.

There's only one problem with this view: It is fiction. With few exceptions, e-learning that runs like clockwork exists only in the minds of predatory suppliers and speakers at conferences. One industry veteran who has evaluated dozens of major companies' efforts says, "When you look under the hood, you find that they have not advanced beyond buying huge libraries of courses and praying for the best."

You may find this very bleak picture shocking. Your research has to deal with things as they are, not a pipedream about what they might be. If your current e-learning is broken, know that you're not alone, and fix it before turning to nice-to-haves.

---

path to a better job, or that e-learning is an effective way to learn. Moreover, your e-learner may not have confidence that *your* version of e-learning is going to work. Maybe even a supervisor or regional manager harbors these doubts.

Sponsors

They may be executives, line managers, technical staff, front-line supervisors, or individual workers. Who are they? How important are they?

You have internal sponsors and detractors at all levels of management, and they're not all concerned at the same things. Return-on-investment is in the eye of the beholder. It's not that you can call up Enron's accountants to cook the books to make the numbers say what you want. It's that people at different levels in an organization have a different take on what constitutes a meaningful "return" (figure 5-2).

Training directors were among the first to bring e-learning into corporations. Compared to instructor-led training, e-learning promised to do the job better, faster, cheaper. The primary focus was on cutting the costs of travel, facilities, and staff. Reduced learning time meant more time on the job. Some companies used e-learning as an excuse to shift learning from work hours to personal time, although most of them soon gave up on this approach.

To their chagrin, training administrators discovered that many of their savings were one-time benefits. Cut $3 million from the travel budget this year by conducting virtual meetings, and next year's budget no longer includes that $3 million. Cutting staff doesn't give you carte blanche to staff up next year. One-time savings only help out one year's budget performance. This is but one reason that line managers have increasing clout as sponsors of e-learning.

Figure 5-2. E-learning benefits: three perspectives.

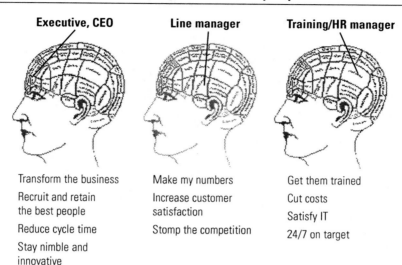

Executive, CEO	Line manager	Training/HR manager
Transform the business	Make my numbers	Get them trained
Recruit and retain the best people	Increase customer satisfaction	Cut costs
Reduce cycle time	Stomp the competition	Satisfy IT
Stay nimble and innovative		24/7 on target

Internal training departments have traditionally focused on building the skills of employees. Ten years ago that worked, but its day is done. People say that only half the people who work for Cisco Systems receive Cisco paychecks. They're referring to members of the Cisco "ecosystem," which includes suppliers, partners, and distributors. Cisco doesn't manufacture much Cisco equipment. The company tends to focus on core operations and outsources everything else, not an uncommon trend.

As corporate management embraces responsibility for the functioning of the entire value chain, partners and customers need training as well. What used to be a corporate HR function has migrated to marketing, operations, and other major functions. For this and other reasons, line managers began to influence e-learning decisions. Their concern was not so much cost cutting as improving the business. Saving money is great, but so is improving customer service or boosting sales. The overriding concerns of unit managers can be stated thus: "Make my numbers, make my numbers, and make my numbers." If e-learning can help, so much the better.

In a few organizations, executive management has embraced e-learning as a way of improving the organization. They want to be more responsive, reduce cycle time, recruit and retain the best people, and transform the business. The principal advocate for this approach, former GE chairman Jack Welch, says, "Learning is at the heart of a company. It is the competitive advantage in an organization," and "Raising the intellect of the company, every day, is what it takes to win."

Will They Buy It?

Guerilla marketer Jay Levinson explains in his article "The Truth About Customers" (1999) why customers buy or do not buy: "People do not buy because marketing is clever, but because marketing strikes a responsive chord in their minds. Customers do not buy because they're being marketed to or sold to. They buy because you help them realize the merits of owning what you offer.

- They buy promises you make. So make them with care.
- They buy your credibility or don't buy if you lack it.
- They buy solutions to their problems.
- They buy you, your people, and your service department.
- They buy other people's opinions of your business.
- They buy expectations based upon your marketing.
- They buy believable claims, not simply honest claims.
- They buy hope for their own and their company's future.
- They buy brand names over strange names.
- They buy the consistency they've seen you exhibit.
- They buy the professionalism of your marketing materials.
- They buy acceptance by others of your goods or services.
- They buy respect for their own ideas and personality.
- They buy your identity as conveyed by your marketing.
- They buy easy access to information about you, offered by your Website.
- They buy comfort, offerings that fit their comfort zone.
- They buy good taste and know it from bad taste."

Go through Levinson's list, using the questions to prod your memory to delineate the good and the bad about your department's brand recognition, brand reputation, and brand loyalty.

Your Brand Image

What's my current reputation with the customers? Do they regard in-house learning with respect or disdain? Do they perceive e-learning as a cost-cutting move that deprives them of the camaraderie and tee-times of live workshops? Research conducted by ASTD and the MASIE Center found that learners base their judgments of the quality of all e-learning on their first e-learning experience. Instead of saying they engaged in e-learning, they say "I took Digital Think" or "I had SkillSoft." If their experience was a good one, future e-learning programs benefit from a halo effect. If their experience was not so good, it will be tough to get them back for another round. You need to know what you're up against.

Early adopters of e-learning often got burned. In a rush to hop on the e-learning train, they bought large course libraries and shoved them on the organization. Course libraries make great economic sense if you assume most people will participate. That's the rub. Most potential learners don't take part. The courses in the library don't map very well to what people need to learn.

The reputation of e-learning may have lost its shine, so getting potential learners excited can be an uphill battle.

Organizational Goals

Your company is not in the e-learning business. It is in the business of satisfying its customers. To make a major contribution to the value of your firm, you must relate learning to accomplishing the corporate mission.

If your company is publicly held, get a copy of the annual report. Read the chairperson's letter. Note the challenges and opportunities there. Study the results of operations. Figure out where the profit comes from.

Your Industry's Environment

Business success is relative. For a corporation to be successful, it must pick a sweet spot in its industry. Perhaps the corporation profits by stomping the competition, or maybe it wins through cooperation with other companies. Or, it may be part of other companies' value chains or a significant node in a business web. No matter the role, an enterprise must be aware of what is going on in its industry.

At the big picture level, the Internet has excellent sources to get you started. For a general snapshot, start with Hoover's industry overviews (http://www .hoovers.com/industry/archive/0,2048,169,00.html). You'll find four dozen overviews of industries such as advertising, aerospace, agriculture, airlines, and so on. The Internet Intelligence Index compiled by Fuld (http://www.fuld .com/i3/) provides in-depth looks at the major industry groups, including links to trade associations, patent information, and stock quotes. For analysis that tells what's going on with specific companies, turn to the archive Websites of the major business magazines, including *Forbes, Business Week,* and *Fortune.*

Macroeconomic Environment

Your enterprise's overall strategic direction was built on an analysis of the firm's relationship to the technology, political, economic, regulatory, and social environment—factors that are beyond its control. Many things outside the corporate walls also affect your e-learning programs. These are volatile times. Everything in our networked world is connected to everything else. Societies around the globe are going through astounding changes. The following are some areas for you to consider:

- In developed countries, the population is aging rapidly. Birthrates are at record lows. People are living longer. In the United States, the bulge of 75 million baby boomers is entering the elderly end of population snake. What will this trend mean in the workforce? It will translate into a workforce that includes more older workers and part-timers.

- Ethnic diversity abounds. The melting pot, which supposedly rendered all Americans the same, has been edged out by a salad bowl of ethnic groups who maintain their individual identities.

- Economies swing to and fro like pendulums. Good times encourage longer-term thinking and humanistic approaches. Learning initiatives are in favor. Theoretical constructs like intellectual capital are translated into action. Bad times foster short-term thinking and excessive control. A so-called "return to basics" is often a codeword for slashing the training budget and axing projects whose payoff is more than a year out. Rational or not, e-learning programs rise and fall with management's perception of the economy.

- Government regulation is on the rise. In the United States, a litigious mindset and zealous enforcement agencies make it necessary for people to understand and comply with regulations on workplace safety, sexual harassment, affirmative action, product safety, and environmental protection. The European Commission is enacting a pan-European set of regulations on consumer protection, fair trade, labeling, and privacy. Globalization mandates more comprehensive trade agreements.

- Generation differences are also significant. How do you develop the talents of learners who find a 15-minute online session about 12 minutes too long?

- Public education in America is producing high-school graduates who cannot read a college textbook. Many have no sense of the sweep of history and can't guess the date of the Civil War within a hundred years. Forty percent of high-school seniors cannot locate France on a map. Corporations may need to offer remedial English classes to acquire literate people for their workforce.

- Web-based services are going to delegate routine work to computers, leaving human beings to exercise their judgment and creativity in larger measure. Extensible markup language (XML) and its brethren enable computers to talk with one another. This development will spark the convergence of jobs, learning, customer relationship management (CRM), enterprise resource planning (ERP), knowledge management, and more.

Trends in E-Learning Technology

What changes in e-learning content, delivery, standards, practices, and suppliers lie ahead? The results of today's decisions will reverberate for years to come. To plan for the future, you need to have a good feel for the direction of e-learning technology. It's likely that the future will see the following developments:

- training merges into work
- learning and knowledge management converge
- e-learning becomes a Web service
- simulation replaces linear subject orientation
- e-learning and other enterprisewide systems converge
- content becomes more industry-specific
- extent of high-quality generic content increases in core areas
- individualized learning prescriptions are based on competency assessments.

ASSEMBLING YOUR FINDINGS

In the old days, when corporations had strategic planning units that peered five years into the future, you'd have bound 100 or more pages of market research findings in an ugly plastic binding and put them on the shelf— no longer. Things change rapidly.

Bringing It All Together

Winning organizations are those that get all the pieces right. Consider, for example, the way Deborah Masten implemented e-learning at JC Penney, a major retailer with a 100-year history, stores in each of the 50 states, and a quarter-million associates.

In 1995, Deborah Masten, then manager of JC Penney's corporate university, faced dwindling budgets and increasing training needs. Flying store managers to headquarters for four days of training was no longer viable. The one-size-fits-all approach made managers prisoners in the classroom. Training back then was an afterthought. When a new business system was complete, the training group would hear about it and then have to play catch-up to publish materials after the fact. As a result, the organization viewed training as out of touch and not really helping the business.

This all changed in 1996 when Masten got management support to build a distance learning program. Finding the learning management systems available at the time too inflexible for its needs, JC Penney developed its own. Each of the 249,000 associates can log into the central system to review what training is required for their position and what they have completed to date; important training assignments rise to the top of the list.

Today, training at JC Penney is entirely paperless. Learning is blended. Training is inseparable from knowledge management. This is the future of e-learning.

You will keep your market research findings in a file that you continually review and update. If your situation isn't changing at least twice a year, you're probably not paying attention. Research and analysis should be a never-ending process, not an annual event.

By now you know enough to begin developing the plans you will be putting into practice. Your research legitimizes what is to come. It is a demonstration that you have done your homework and are putting the needs of the organization and its people ahead of parochial departmental needs. A great way to communicate the comprehensive nature of your findings is to display them as a mind map (figure 5-3).

Figure 5-3. Using a mind map to communicate your market research findings.

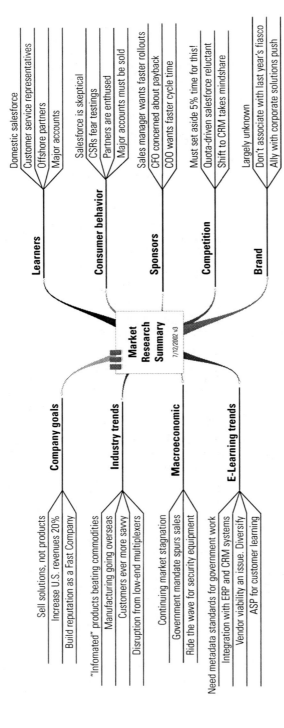

For additional information on creating mind maps, see
http://www.InternetTime.com/visual
http://www.peterussell.com/Mindmaps/HowTo.html and
http://www.jcu.edu.au/studying/services/studyskills/mindmap/howto.html.

YOUR TURN

Using worksheet 5-1 as a guide, summarize your market research findings in two to five pages.

Worksheet 5-1. Your market research findings.

Assemble your market research findings, using this checklist to ensure that you haven't overlooked anything.

Market Research Topics

☐ Your consumers, the learners (attach your target consumer descriptions)
☐ Consumer behavior (what it takes to win their loyalty)
☐ Competitors for consumers' attention
☐ Sponsors and what they are looking for
☐ Your brand image
☐ Organizational goals
☐ Your industry's environment
☐ Macroeconomic environment
☐ Trends in e-learning technology

After you pull together all the materials, post your findings on your intranet. Distribute copies. Ask people at all levels if your research findings jive with their understanding of the situation. The best way to head off conflict down the road is to leave everything out in the open.

Successful e-learning initiatives derive support from multiple levels. Without sponsorship, your efforts are doomed. For each level of sponsorship you are counting on, check off on worksheet 5-2 the items that apply, adding any items you deem vital to your organization.

Worksheet 5-2. Primary ROI drivers for your e-learning.

Cut Costs, Boost Efficiency	Meet Business Objectives	Improve the Organization
☐ Slash travel budget	☐ Become competent sooner	☐ Transform the business
☐ Reduce time away from the job	☐ Improve customer service	☐ Increase flexibility
☐ Automate instruction	☐ Increase sales	☐ Stay ahead of competition
☐ Reduce training positions	☐ Train customers	☐ Add to human capital
☐ Accelerate training	☐ Expand global reach	☐ Reduce turnover
☐ Keep up with demand for knowledge	☐ Reduce cycle time	☐ Boost morale
	☐ Beat competitors	☐ Foster innovation
		☐ Share best practices

6

Applying Marketing Design

You won't find *marketing design* in marketing textbooks or hear it in lecture halls at business schools because marketing is often taught using a more regimented approach. As you have been working through this book, you have been gathering the information you need to come up with a marketing plan that will help you successfully implement e-learning. It is time to think out of the box and be creative to create a plan that works for your organization.

THE DESIGN DISCIPLINE

Using the metaphor of design in marketing emphasizes the fact that this is a creative endeavor, but one with a purpose. The best marketing design is that which is perfectly appropriate to what we are trying to accomplish. The design metaphor also makes time-tested maxims available:

- Less is more.
- Form follows function.
- Everything should be made as simple as possible, but no simpler.

For example, Shaker furniture is renowned for its beauty, balance, and functionality. Shaker design holds true to these guidelines. The furniture is well made, honest, and functional. Let the same be true of your e-learning, and let your marketing reflect that fact.

THE ELEMENTS OF MARKETING DESIGN

A successful e-learning marketing design is a balance of three factors:

- a brand that creates a reputation that keeps customers coming back and attracts new customers

■ market segmentation that optimizes results by leveraging the most appropriate groups of customers

■ a position that places your product in the "sweet spot" in the customer's mind.

Figure 6-1 offers an example of an e-learning marketing design based on a mind map. The rest of the chapter will offer you the chance to do marketing design exercises on brand, segmentation, and positioning.

Branding Your E-Learning

No doubt you're already very familiar with branding from your personal experience as a shopper. A brand is a "name, term, sign, symbol, or design, or a combination of these intended to identify the products or services of one seller or group of sellers and to differentiate them from those of competitors. A brand is a seller's promise to deliver consistently a specific set of features, benefits, and services to buyers" (Kotler, 1999). Brands convey benefits, values, and personality.

Certainly you know of Coca-Cola, McDonald's, Porsche, and Sony—some of the world's best-known brands. What associations do you make? Do you like some of these brands a great deal? Do you trust them to deliver a good product? Would you pay more for something sporting one of these brand names than a similar generic product? If one of these companies brought out a new product, would you consider buying it?

No, you don't have to invest billions of dollars, as these companies do, to promote your e-learning brand. Nonetheless, creating an in-house brand for your e-learning can help you generate more loyal customers and keep them coming back for more. The point is that you have greater e-learning success by putting forth a consistent, identifiable image, and a similar message.

Marketing Is Building a Brand

In the early 1980s, Al Ries and Jack Trout wrote a brilliant pamphlet to publicize their advertising agency. The duo mailed out thousands of free copies of "Positioning: The Battle for Your Mind." The pamphlet grew into a best-selling book and profoundly affected the practice of marketing. Ries and Trout went on to write several groundbreaking books on marketing, including *The 22 Immutable Laws of Marketing: Violate Them at Your Own Risk* (1994).

Flowing from the laws of marketing are the laws of branding. Here is a quote from *The 22 Immutable Laws of Branding: How to Build a Product or Service Into a World-Class Brand* (Ries & Ries, 1998) that is worth remembering: "In the consumer's mind, there is no difference between a company or product name and a brand name. Marketing is building a brand in the mind of the prospect. If you can build a powerful brand, you will have a powerful marketing program. If you can't, then all the advertising, fancy packaging, sales promotion, and public relations in the world won't help you achieve your objective."

Figure 6-1. The marketing plan revealed as a mind-mapping exercise.

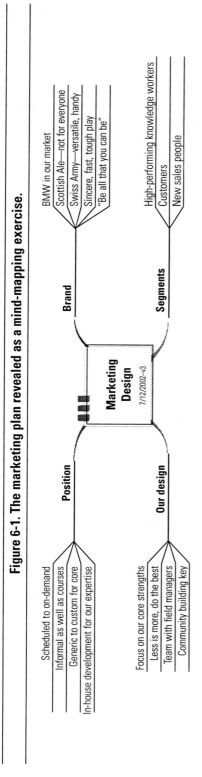

For example, every flier, brochure, memorandum, giveaway, and computer screen from the Learning Center at Aspect Communications carries its meaningful icon (figure 6-2). The icon demonstrates the pride the Learning Center has in its work. It implies that "the quality goes in before the logo goes on."

Your e-learning brand differentiates your e-learning from the general marketplace and all the distractions your learner faces. If training in general has a "nonessential" reputation at your organization, a brand can help demonstrate

Figure 6-2. Even Post-It notes and Koozie beverage insulators carry the memorable icon that is part of the Learning Center's brand.

Koozie

Post-It Notes

Source: Reprinted with permission from the Learning Center, Aspect Communications. 2002.

how your e-learning product is different, better, and more exciting than the other products. And, just as important, an in-house brand makes it easier to create brand extensions, that is, to put other learning opportunities and interventions into an existing program.

Building Your Brand Identity. Despite what you've read, you still may be wondering why building brand identity is important. Brand identity specifies your promise to your customers and creates a value proposition that involves functional, emotional, or self-expressed benefits. Brand image is the way your customers see you now. See table 6-1 for a bit of the "ying" and "yang" of brand identity and image. In the case of e-learning, you care because you want learners to come back. If you focus on brand identity, brand image will follow.

Creating Effective Brands. Novice marketers often create brands that reflect *product* characteristics, but astute marketers look more to lasting *emotional* benefits. Remember, brands created with product characteristics assume that buyers make rational decisions, which is rarely the case when customers buy a soft drink, diamond ring, or an e-learning experience.

Your E-Learning Brand Personality. Although implementing and marketing e-learning are not the same as branding a national consumer product, you can take some lessons from these national brands. A recent study of 60 top brands revealed that sincerity (Campbell's and Hallmark), excitement (Porsche, Absolut, Benetton), competence (American Express, CNN, IBM), sophistication (Lexus, Mercedes, Revlon), and ruggedness (Levi's, Marlboro, Nike) accounted for an astounding 93 percent of the differences between brands (Aaker, 1995).

As you plan your marketing for e-learning, think about what personality will appeal most to your customers. See table 6-2 for some help in thinking

Table 6-1. Comparing brand image and brand identity.

Brand Image	Brand Identity
What you've got	Where you want to be
Looking back	Looking ahead
Appearance	Reality
Superficial	Enduring
Others' view	Your desire
Passive	Active

Table 6-2. Organizational aspects of your brand identity.

Innovative	Concerned about customers	Successful
High-tech	Substantial	Credible
Trustworthy	Profit-driven	In-the-know

through your organization's personality. Consider the brand identity reflected by your organization and its culture, and think about how these attributes can be incorporated into your brand identity.

Create an E-Learning Slogan. The purpose of this book is not to educate you in the general principles of marketing, but you can take a lesson from familiar marketing campaigns. Table 6-3 lists some famous slogans, jingles, and icons from the magazine *Advertising Age.* You probably do not need to spend an inordinate amount of time developing these elements, but thinking of your e-learning brand in a professional way is very important for the success of your e-learning implementation effort.

Marketing to the Right Segment

Market analysis pioneer Daniel Yankelovich says, "Once you discover the most useful ways of segmenting a market, you have produced the beginnings of a sound marketing strategy." Yet, the concept of segmentation is deceptively simple. Segments are nothing more than chunks of the market you intend to treat differently from others.

If you're marketing beer, you might focus most heavily on 18- to 30-year-old males, a group that tends to consume more beer than others. Because this segment of the market regularly spends football season in front of the television, you place the bulk of your advertising dollars there. If you're selling flavored lipstick, you would probably focus on teenaged girls and run ads in teen magazines.

Marketers frequently target segments defined by income, purchase history, magazine subscriptions, lifestyle, and home ownership. Mass marketers have found it economically worthwhile to profile people's backgrounds in great detail. How do they find out who falls into which segment? Neural-net programs ceaselessly farm "data warehouses" of customer transactions in search of patterns that can lead to new and more lucrative segmentation. These virtual warehouses contain information on estimated income, credit records, home value, mortgage burden, make/model/year of cars owned, major purchases going back five years, magazine subscriptions, email addresses, number and age

Slogans	Jingles	Icons
Diamonds are forever (DeBeers)	You deserve a break today (McDonald's Restaurants)	The Marlboro Man (Marlboro cigarettes)
Just do it (Nike)	Be all that you can be (U.S. Army)	Ronald McDonald (McDonald's Restaurants)
The pause that refreshes (Coca-Cola)	Pepsi Cola hits the spot (Pepsi Cola)	The Jolly Green Giant (Green Giant vegetables)
Tastes great, less filling (Miller Lite)	M'm! M'm! Good! (Campbell's)	Betty Crocker (Betty Crocker food products)
We try harder (Avis)	See the U.S.A. in your Chevrolet (General Motors)	The Energizer Bunny (Eveready Energizer batteries)
Good to the last drop (Maxwell House)	I wish I was an Oscar Meyer wiener (Oscar Meyer)	The Pillsbury Doughboy (assorted Pillsbury foods)
Breakfast of champions (Wheaties)	Double your pleasure, double your fun (Wrigley's Doublemint gum)	Aunt Jemima (Aunt Jemima pancake mixes and syrup)
Does she...or doesn't she? (Clairol)	Winston tastes good like a cigarette should (Winston)	The Michelin Man (Michelin tires)
When it rains, it pours (Morton salt)	It's the real thing (Coca-Cola)	Tony the Tiger (Kellogg's Sugar Frosted Flakes)
Where's the beef (Wendy's Restaurants)	A little dab'll do ya (Brylcreem)	Elsie (Borden dairy products)

Table 6-3. Famous slogans, jingles, and icons.

of children, bank accounts, and credit cards. Even though assembling such extensive, detailed customer dossiers costs marketers a great deal of money, in the long run, they'll be more astute in assessing how much they invest in developing certain segments as customers.

Remember, the whole point of segmentation is to focus on groups you intend to treat differently from others. While you won't need information about learners' mortgage balances or wine-drinking preferences, but you can use market segmentation to slice the market into chunks for marketing your e-learning. For one thing, you can define different levels of service for different segments. Aspect's Kara Underwood and her team deliver two distinct types of e-learning:

1. custom courses that are strategically aligned, very powerful, capable of having an organization-wide impact
2. catalog courses, which are best suited for individuals, and are likely to enjoy widespread participation if they are part of an overall solution, for example, certification or an instructor-led course

What groups would you single out for special treatment in e-learning? Who might drop off your interest list entirely? Remember, the whole point of segmentation is to focus on groups you intend to treat differently from others. Think about some potential segments as you implement and market e-learning.

Market segmentation must be appropriate for your organization's environment. Table 6-4 lists some potential segmentation factors, but remember, only *you* can judge what's appropriate for *your* organization. The checkmarks and Xs represent the authors' best guesses at what your organization's needs might be.

As you identify different segments of your universe of customers, pay special attention to where you expect to get the most bang for your buck. Segmentation is about treating people differently, not the same.

Segmentation and the Restaurant Analogy. Compare old-style training versus your e-learning initiative to two different dining experiences (table 6-5). You could eat in a stuffy 1950s restaurant, where the overly rich, expensive food is served in courses by a tuxedo-clad waiter, or you could dine in a modern, upscale bistro that offers a relaxed buffet where you can pick and choose just what you like at your leisure.

Where would you rather eat? Or learn? After all, learning is food for thought.

Putting Segmentation Concepts to Use. Training directors at one time had a mandate to provide consistent, equal offerings to everyone in the organization, but today's concept of the learning bistro views your audience as segments that need to be treated differently.

Consider the problem faced by one German company. With 45,000 employees at 40 production sites, this company is the largest independent specialist for transmission and chassis technology worldwide. The company's partners expect its people to be competent with new technologies, so it is now aiming to make all employees competent Internet users.

Think about how you might solve this company's marketing and implementation problems based on the following situation:

- Employees are in all stages of life, with all kinds of educational background, and have very different levels of motivation and experience in using computers and the Internet.
- Less than a third of all workplaces are equipped with computers.
- The company has a culture of consensus rather than command-and-control, so employees need to be convinced of the benefits, rather than ordered what to do from above.

If the goal at the end of the day is having all employees certified as qualified Web users, how would you go about the task of marketing and implementing this e-learning effort?

Table 6-4. Some ideas about the relative importance of various segmentation factors in marketing e-learning.

Segmentation Factor	Examples	Relative Importance for E-Learning Marketing (number of ✓s indicates increasing value; number of Xs indicates decreasing value)	Explanation
Tenure	Novice, apprentice, old hand	✓	Tenure is important for identifying who needs basic information about how the company functions. Also, old hands are often the least served and most needy when it comes to learning.
Rank	Employee, supervisor, executive	✓	You segment a market because you intend to treat the segments differently. You're going to offer different e-learning opportunities to these groups. If for nothing else, you can get more budget per capita the higher you go in the organization.
Role in the Organization	Customer, supplier, channel partner, employee	✓✓	Of course this segment matters. You're not going to share confidential information with outsiders, are you? Probably the importance of customer and partner learning is part of the overall organization's objectives.
Personal Transportation	Bicycle, motorcycle, car, sport-utility vehicle, truck	✗	Who cares? This is not a valuable segmentation.
Learning Style	Aural, oral, kinesthetic	✗	You think people learn best when presented learning opportunities in their preferred style. True. But, usually it's more expensive than it's worth to provide multiple versions of learning experience for different learning styles. Besides, offering a variety of methods isn't market segmentation because everyone is presented with the same choices.

(Continued on page 70)

Table 6-4. Some ideas about the relative importance of various segmentation factors in marketing e-learning (continued).

Segmentation Factor	Examples	Relative Importance for E-Learning Marketing (number of ✓s indicates increasing value; number of Xs indicates decreasing value)	Explanation
Myers-Briggs Type Indicator (MBTI) Score	I/E, N/S, F/T, P/J	X	(Learning style revisited. Also, the MBTI instrument assessment isn't validated as a definitive indicator of learning style, and you probably don't have everyone's MBTI scores anyway.
Performance	Average, superstar	✓✓	Among knowledge workers, this factor can be vital. Think of the outliers, the crème de la crème. These people are the major source of corporate innovation. Although the ROI of learning depends to a certain extent on the learner's degree of freedom, a high performer may add 100 times the value of his or her mediocre peer. Imagine a spectrum of workers, arrayed by how well they perform. Provide training. Often you'll receive the following: —50% gain from a worker in the lowest 25% —200% gain from an average worker —500% gain from a worker in the top 25% —10,000% gain from a top 1% worker
Personality	Inquisitive, outgoing, reserved	X	There's no feasible way to measure this factor. Also, it's unclear what you'd do with the information if you had it. Such factors do not scale.
Technology Adoption	Enthusiast, early adopter, early majority, late majority, diehard	✓	The first wave of learners is tolerant risk-takers, and the bulk who follow are picky go-alongs. If you work it right, you can get these groups to self-select.

Job Title and Competencies	Job titles and required/desired competencies from job descriptions	✓	Assuming you've got a reliable learning management system that incorporates competencies, it's great to set personal learning goals.
Gender	Male, female	*xxx*	*Why?* In all likelihood it's not even legal to make professional development decisions based on gender. Or race. And it doesn't make much difference anyway
Age	—	*xxx*	Same story as for gender. What's age got to do with it?
Generation	Mature, baby boomer, Generation X, Generation Y	✓✓	People in different generations learn differently. Generation tracks age but not precisely. The calendar defines age; the cultural experiences shared with one's peers define generation. Gen Y has body piercings and does homework in front of the television, the Web, five live-chat sessions, perhaps a group game, and a telephone call. Baby boomers are repelled by piercings and need isolation to concentrate. This factor is critical to segmentation, for it calls for multiple paths to learning.
Past E-Learning Experience	Novice, good experience with e-learning, unfavorable experience with e-learning	✓	People assume all e-learning is going to be like their one e-learning experience. If a prior e-learning experience left a bad taste in the learner's mouth, it will take some selling to get him or her to come back for another dose. If this is the e-learner's first experience online, it's worth the extra effort to make sure the first learning experience is a good one.

Table 6-5. The restaurant analogy for positioning your e-learning.

Training Restaurant 1950	E-Learning Bistro 2002
Nothing available à la carte	Smorgasbord; choose what you wish
All meals take at least 50 minutes	Stay as long (or little) as you like
Limited menu; the "chef" addresses only basic skills	Broad selection of food for everyone's tastes
Nothing prepared to order	Chef prepares dishes to order
No self-service; the waiter delivers the meal when it's ready	Salad bar, desserts, and other items are self-service
No take-out; learn in the classroom, not on the job	Eat at the table, at your desk, at home, while commuting
Unneeded fat; e.g., travel, rehashing of what's known, overkill	Less fat and more fuel; more signal and less noise
No substitutions; you eat what everyone else eats	Menu is experimental, seasonal, accommodating
Wine choice is "red" or "white" and of unknown origin	Waiter can describe six boutique chardonnays for you
Frozen ingredients for convenience of the kitchen	Attractive, wholesome, fresh ingredients draw you in
No eating between meals; learn only in class	Eat when you're hungry, open 24/7, have a snack
Menu is "conventional" and, therefore, out of step with the times	Menu changes frequently; there's always something new to try

How Generations Affect Marketing Efforts. *Rocking the Ages,* the book that introduced the subject of generational marketing, begins with an ancient proverb: "Men resemble the times more than they do their fathers" (Smith & Clurman, 1997). Members of a generation are shaped by the shared experiences of their time. Everyone is aware of the differences between baby boomers, Generation Xers, the millennial generation, and the other generational labels that have been given to different age groups. Thinking about the differences in generations is important as you put together your marketing and implementation plan for e-learning.

Aspect Learning Center, a Great E-Learning Bistro

Kara Underwood's team at the Learning Center at Aspect Communications lives and breathes the bistro philosophy: Choose what you want and stay as long as you like. When she arrived in at Aspect in May 2000, sales training consisted of three stultifying weeks of PowerPoint presentations in one darkened room. Her mandate was to reduce time to productivity by 10 percent.

Her team created a blended, holistic, mentored program that cut time to productivity by 37 percent while cutting costs in half and chopping time out of the field by 60 percent. By relegating product, tools, and process knowledge and technical training to e-learning, Aspect trimmed a 15-day experience to just over four days of largely interactive application practice.

New hires in sales at Aspect Communications are assigned a seasoned mentor who observes their behavior and guides their development. The new hire receives checklists of development steps for the first 30, 60, and 90 days. An item might be a unit of training or a joint sales call. A learning management system tracks accomplishments by individual and registers sign-off by the mentor.

Aspect Communications has replicated this e-learning model throughout the organization. When Aspect was shifting its corporate direction from hardware to software, training was needed for the salesforce, channel partners, and customers. Rather than reinvent the wheel (and burn out subject matter experts), Aspect leveraged subject matter expertise and project management time by implementing a unified e-learning curriculum with multiple versions. The in-house salesforce receives the comprehensive product training curriculum; channel partners get the same (minus competitive information); and customers receive an e-learning overview followed by the technical instructor-led curriculum.

By focusing on the precise needs of key segments, Aspect was able to deliver significant results at reduced cost.

Generation Y (those born between 1977 and 1995) is so different from the baby boomer generation that it will stand our concept of training on its head. Gen Yers process information in parallel; while doing homework online, they may be listening to music and conversing in five simultaneous chat windows. They are easily bored. The Gen Yers describe themselves as optimistic, confident, ambitious, committed, and empowered. They appreciate the value of learning as a way to meet their goals. However, they need incredible amounts of reinforcement, having been brought up with video games that provide 60 to 100 times more reinforcement than what previous generations considered normal.

Take a look at the way Don Tapscott (1998) describes the learning styles of Gen Y. He observes that the confident Gen Y is emotionally and intellectually open. He expects many barriers to workplace collaboration to melt. Gen Y is likely to be the most color-blind, gender-neutral, and socially classless group in history. They value others' contributions. Couple this with a pragmatic urge to take action and you have the perfect seedbed for collaboration. Networking comes naturally.

How do you want your e-learning to be perceived relative to competing uses of your consumers' time? To other means of professional development? To other ways of learning to serve *their own* customers better?

The Effect of Cultural Differences. Yeoh Phee Guan of the Knowledge House relates that unrealistic expectations and a poor fit with cultural norms retarded the growth of e-learning in Malaysia.

A couple years ago, some e-learning advocates declared that Malaysia was at the threshold of an "e-learning revolution." But, the revolution hasn't happened. E-learning solution providers sprouted, but there were not many e-learners. In fact, some e-learning companies couldn't survive.

What barriers to e-learning existed? First, there were no Malaysian "Paul Reveres" to excite the people to move, to take the plunge into e-learning. In addition, Malaysians have been used to a mode of learning whereby they were closely coached; self-directed learning was not popular.

The mode of learning in this country has been very examination-oriented. A learner is gauged by his or her public examination results. Other modes of assessment do not show off a learner's capabilities as much as the results of their public examinations. Technological limitations—narrow bandwidth, limited PC penetration in the population—have also slowed adoption of e-learning.

For e-learning to catch on, solution providers will have to use careful segmentation practices.

Positioning E-Learning in the Mind of Your Customer

Segmentation dealt with identifying the people in your target markets. Positioning is about what's in their heads. As Jack Trout (2000) puts it: Positioning is "not what you do to the product, but what you do to the mind." For example, people perceive BMW automobiles as sporty. Volvos are considered safe. Cadillacs represent the epitome of luxury to many people.

Position is all about place. In fact, that's what the dictionary says *position* means. Positioning involves putting your product in a context within the customer's head. Marketers do this through analogy and concept maps.

Mental Maps. What's the best way to find what position you're in? Use a map. Marketing maps are not topographical; they're maps of concepts. Conceptual maps can help you think through how you want to change the nature of learning in your organization. Maps are also useful for explaining your plans to others.

Let's plot the location of a company's primary training on a sample concept map. Assume that most of their current training consists of instructor-led workshops on in-house products and procedures. It appears on figure 6-3 as the area marked "current."

The real value of a map comes from showing where you're going. In this case, assume that your mandate is to cut delivery cost, provide information to new hires as soon as they come on board, and instruct workers in your company's Asian offices. To accomplish these goals, you intend to videotape the live sessions, chunk it into learning objects, and stream it on demand over your corporate intranet. The goals appear on figure 6-3 as the area marked "future."

The dimensions you choose should reflect the issues that are most important in your organization. For example, you might choose any two of these:

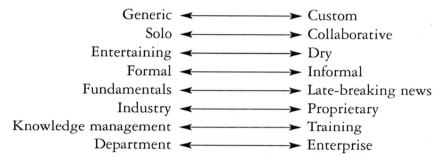

Figures 6-4 and 6-5 offer a couple more examples of mental mapping exercises. See if you agree with the interpretations that follow each. Compare the journeys described on the maps to what you're trying to accomplish.

Figure 6-3. A mental map for positioning e-learning.

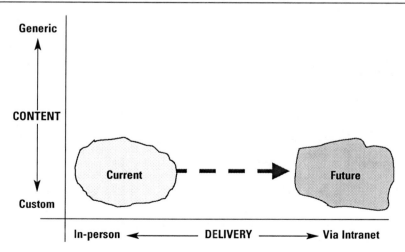

Figure 6-4. Mental mapping: becoming a solution provider.

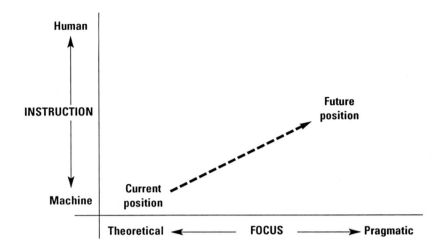

INTERPRETATION: Sales training at this company had consisted primarily of generic sales skills modules purchased as part of a license agreement with a major supplier. The training was both cheap and scalable—training delivery was totally automated and "already paid for" as part of a license for IT skills. Because the modules did not describe selling situations in the firm's industry, most people failed to learn from them. With competition heating up, the firm wanted to reposition itself as a solution provider rather than a seller of point solutions. The company is moving to a combination of presentations delivered by salesforce superstars and a high-end consultative selling package with field exercises.

Figure 6-5. Mental mapping: moving from advance training to just-in-time training.

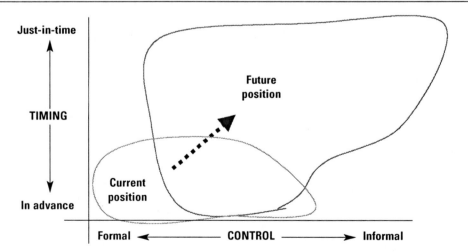

INTERPRETATION: You may find it more meaningful to map areas where your e-learning is taking place and where you want to go. Here you see a firm that's moving from formal (classroom) training in advance to training when you need it (which might be class). The just-in-time training will be either clips from courses rerun on demand (formal) or channels open 24/7 for inquiry, coaching, and true mentoring.

Mindfulness in Your E-Learning Marketing. Part of your e-learning implementation plan should consider how your e-learning courses will be viewed by your customers. Is your e-learning authoritative or loose? Gospel or gossip? Definitive or open-ended? This perception is more important than you might think.

Ellen Langer (1990; 1998) addresses the concept of mindful learning. In an experiment, professors at one college handed out a paper on urban sociology, telling students they would have a few minutes to read it, after which they would be tested on the material. Another group of students were given the same paper and the same instructions, with one addition bit of information—they were told that the content of the paper might not reflect the real situation.

Surprisingly, the second "skeptical group" achieved higher scores because, according to the researchers, uncertainty engages the mind. When people mull something over and test it for fit with what they already know, they are putting it in context—finding a place for it in their network of thoughts and memories. In contrast, when people are told "This is it," they often simply put the information into short-term memory. Without a longer-term connection to what they already know, the idea quickly fades.

You can use this concept to help in your implementation and marketing of e-learning. Rather than position an e-learning experience as absolute truth, you could tell learners that the content is the latest thinking on the subject and ask the learners to look for places the material does not apply.

Years ago, a major manufacturer developed a prototype for technical training using handheld home videocameras. Shot on the factory floor, the videos were the jerky, blurred productions you'd expect. In testing, however, the manufacturer discovered that the crude videos were more credible with trainees than the slick studio productions modeled after them. Cheaper and more realistic, the home videos were more effective.

Developing Your "Elevator Pitch." Here's the situation: A senior executive from your company boards your elevator. It's just the two of you. She asks what's up with the e-learning program. You have a 30-second elevator ride to describe the essence of your value proposition. What you say is your elevator pitch. Better make it good.

Experts advise you to

- Be brief. The exec may get off the elevator early.
- Start with a line that grabs the executive's attention.
- Be enthusiastic.
- Avoid jargon.
- Make it conversational.

- Tell what problem you're solving.
- Highlight the benefits of your solution.
- Make your solution tangible.

Here's a sample pitch. This one has some rough edges, so don't mimic it:

> "Our people need to be able to respond almost immediately to new opportunities, competitive threats, and changing customer expectations. That's tough in today's world of incessant demands and information overload. My group is creating electronic support to help our workers keep up with the pace of change and provide the service we promise our customers. We aim to help all XYZ employees become more innovative, flexible, and successful. If you're interested, I could give you a short presentation on our progress this afternoon."

PUT IT ALL TOGETHER

You've explored the image you want your brand to project. You've researched your environment. You've segmented the market to identify the most profitable targets. You've thought about how you want to position your e-learning. Now you're going to distill and consolidate your conclusions.

You may find it more fun and productive to do this activity with a team. You might want to invite sponsors or members of a training council as well. This enjoyable process brings many issues to the table and helps people create a unified vision.

Preparation is easy. First, make sure everyone reviews your analysis and findings to-date. Second, gather magazines, junk mail, and brochures, and cut out lots of interesting pictures, especially of people. You may end up with such diverse images as

- a boy pointing to a blackboard
- Manhattan skyscrapers with ersatz network connections
- cartoon of a large fish about to eat a smaller fish
- woman pointing to a flowchart on a wall-sized display
- Tiger Woods smiling
- groups of rock climbers
- Matthew Broderick sitting on a 12-foot-high stack of books
- a fireman looking thoughtfully into his PC at the fire station.

Now you're ready to convene the meeting. Explain that the objective will be to give voice to your elevator pitch. Briefly review your market research and your tentative conclusions about your brand, target segments, and position.

Spread out the pictures on a conference table. Instruct each person to choose three or four pictures that represent their hopes and plans for developing, marketing, and implementing the e-learning under consideration. Appoint someone to take notes during the next part of the meeting.

When people have made their choices, ask each in turn to hold up a picture, describe its subject matter, and explain how it relates to your e-learning identity. Your group's culture will determine whether people comment after each picture or hold their discussion until everyone has had a turn. Cycle back around until the ideas stop flowing.

At this point, you can bring out a pair of scissors, a large sheet of butcher paper or poster board, and a jug of rubber cement. As a group exercise, assemble a collage that captures the consensus of the group. Discuss what feels right and what needs work. Take a picture of the output with a digital camera and post the results to a Website to serve as both a historical record and a way to explain things to others.

You'll have the chance in worksheet 6-4 to build on all your marketing research, design, promotion, and brainstorming to create your elevator pitch. Your pitch should describe your brand identity, target markets, and positioning. These words are your catalyst for all that follows. Practice the pitch until it is second nature. Use it to preface any conversations you have with corporate executives.

YOUR TURN

You have seen how a successful e-learning marketing design is a balance of brand identity, market segmentation, and positioning. Now it's your turn to apply these elements as you develop your marketing plan—a plan that will become an integral part of your implementation action plan. Start with worksheet 6-1.

Worksheet 6-1. Define your brand identity.

1. What do you want your organization and services to be known for?

2. What is your functional value proposition to your consumers?

3. What is your emotional value proposition to your consumers?

4. How will your brand identity give meaning to the lives of your customers?

5. Just as a brand identity may reflect a person (personality), it may reflect an organization and its culture. What attributes of your organization might you incorporate into your brand identity? Check off any that seem particularly appropriate:

   ☐ Innovative
   ☐ High-tech
   ☐ Trustworthy
   ☐ Concerned about customers
   ☐ Substantial
   ☐ Profit-driven
   ☐ Successful
   ☐ Credible
   ☐ In-the-know

Now, put your imagination to work on worksheet 6-2.

Worksheet 6-2. Use your brand imagination.

Concerning your brand identity going forward:

If your e-learning were a beer, which one would it be?	
If your e-learning were a car . . .	
If your e-learning were a college . . .	
If your e-learning were a book . . .	
If your e-learning were a game . . .	

That was fun, wasn't it? Now jot down why you made those choices. What do they say about your brand identity?

It's time for some serious work on your marketing plan now. Use worksheet 6-3 as your guide.

Worksheet 6-3. Your e-learning brand identity.

1. Provide the following elements of your brand identity:

   Brand name:

   Brand icon or logo:

   A few core values:

2. What are your target markets and why did you choose them?

(continued on page 82)

Worksheet 6-3. Your e-learning brand identity (continued).

3. Which market segments will you focus on? List four or five.

   1.

   2.

   3.

   4.

   5.

4. Plot the current position of your training efforts and where you want to take them, using any dimensions you deem appropriate. Review the examples in figures 6-4 and 6-5 for guidance.

Now, develop and hone your elevator pitch. Review the advice and the example pitch provided in the chapter. Give it a try, using worksheet 6-4.

Worksheet 6-4. Your elevator pitch.

1. Draft an elevator pitch for your e-learning. Write it here:

2. Describe the important aspects of your marketing plan that came up during the discussion of your elevator pitch.

7

Launching Your E-Learning Marketing and Implementation Plan

This chapter offers practical advice for using the principles you have learned in this book to implement and market e-learning in your organization. You will find examples of what has worked (or failed) in organizations along with some ideas on next steps to take.

The first part of the chapter deals with motivation, overcoming obstacles, timing things right, and looking out for the learners' long-term interests. The second part describes how promotion works and elements you'll use in developing your "package."

CUSTOMER WANTS AND NEEDS AND MOTIVATION

The strongest motivation is internal. You cannot force learners to learn. Positive reinforcement and intrinsic motivation work. Here are some pointers to help you create material for marketing and implementing e-learning in your organization:

- *Relevance:* How do you create learning that people will clamor to take part in? Make it relevant to their needs. Answer the fundamental question: "What's in it for me?" Make your e-learning relevant and state your value proposition clearly.
- *Community:* Whenever possible, create groups to discuss what they're learning, to help each understand, and to keep things on track. IBM's Karen Kocher describes bringing groups together to discuss what they have learned each week. Participants would talk about favorite parts, both face-to-face and networked collaborative chat.

An Expert Comments on Marketing E-Learning

According to Don O'Guin, global manager of Pharmacia, "Marketing implies promotion to many people, but the way I see it, fielding the right product (learning) to satisfy one's customers (learners) is more important."

O'Guin found that offering learning aligned with the organization's core values and mirroring the competencies required to exhibit those values sells itself. Pharmacia Corporation identified its "best management behaviors" and mapped them to e-learning from DDI and SkillSoft. Managers now have a valuable global tool to suggest practical steps in their subordinates' development plans. The approach is driven by individual need for development rather than artificial demand.

- *Value:* Make your value proposition clear. If e-learning is a pathway to promotion, growth, or a better performance review, ensure that learners make the connection.
- *Participation:* People enjoy trying new things. They thrive on attaining mastery by doing. Give people an opportunity to create, to express, and to be themselves, and they're likely to come back for more.

REMOVE THE OBSTACLES TO LEARNING

If you put up enough hurdles, the best content in the world will fail to attract an audience. Here are some common obstacles that you should watch out for as you develop your e-learning, marketing, and implementation plan:

- *No help or helpers:* Cut off sources of frustration early on. Show your picture. Give learners a help-line telephone number to call. Provide an online suggestion box. Recruit former learners as learning guides for novices. Only a quarter of employees at Sun Microsystems completed courses that were pure self-study; three times that many finished programs complemented by mentors and peer discussion. Put people in the program and make it easy for lost souls to find them.
- *Wrong size:* Some online universities have tried to sell business courses to corporations. Most have crashed and burned because no one in business wants to devote a semester to learning something; few will want to spend even an hour. For most situations, five or 10 minutes is a long time. Supply e-learning in as small a chunk as possible.
- *Insufficient time:* The ability to learn anytime, anywhere is great if you have time to spare and a quiet place to reflect. In the early days, many an ROI argument was based on shifting learning from time on the job to employee time at home. For the mass of workers, this devalues

training and plays the learner for a sucker. Results are spotty. If the organization values learning, it must make time for it. There is no such thing as a free lunch.

- *Gratuitous eye candy:* A learner under time pressure has little patience with elements incorporated into e-learning because they are cute. What one learner finds amusing, the next will find inappropriate.
- *Poor design:* Tedious, linear, illogical presentations that are irrelevant forays into history, vocabulary, obsolete practice, and irrelevancies make learners tune out. Use a variety of modes and methods to keep learners engaged.

GETTING LEARNERS TO REMEMBER

Learners intuitively know that there's something wrong with weeklong workshops. A great deal of material is covered, but when it comes time to apply the lessons, all those notes have turned into useless one-liners. This fact is not a startling new revelation; it's been known since at least the 1930s. Take a look at table 7-1 to see just how long your learners will remember a lesson.

Table 7-1. How long learners recall material.

Time From First Learning	Percentage of Material Remembered	Percentage of Material Forgotten
After 1 day	54%	46%
After 7 days	35%	65%
After 14 days	21%	79%
After 21 days	18%	82%
After 28 days	19%	81%
After 63 days	17%	83%

THINKING FOR THE LONGER TERM

Learners are smart enough to know whether you're looking out for their interests or simply going through the motions. One of the greatest gifts you can impart to learners is the power to continuously improve the way they learn for the rest of their lives. Learning itself is a skill. It can be examined, practiced, and improved. Fewer things can leverage the time, professionalism, and enjoyment of knowledge workers more than helping them learn how to learn better.

For an individual, learning how to learn—meta-learning—improves performance. It includes such things as the following:

- self-empowerment (attitude, self-confidence, and understanding)
- choices about the best way to learn (individual, group, debate, triage, and so forth) and access to the best sources of information
- personal knowledge management (capturing and reflecting on one's toolkit)
- forming powerful relationships with mentors, colleagues, and information sources
- continuous reflection (double loop, goal of self-improvement)
- a reinforcing learning environment.

For an organization, improvement is influenced by culture, organizational support, managerial roles, and other areas that extend beyond what any individual can do. These areas include a supportive organizational culture, a sense of community, networking and communication infrastructure, a respect for learning and its ROI, mentorship, and implementation of programs with sound meta-learning design.

Corporations are seeking meta-learning to spark innovation, decrease cycle time, build lasting customer relationships, lower turnover, increase organizational agility, and forge competitive advantage. A few visionary organizations are infusing their cultures with dedication to continual improvement in these areas, making them self-sustaining (Cross & Quinn, 2002).

PROMOTION

Now that you understand some of the basic concepts about why and how learners learn, it is time to put this knowledge to work. This section will give you a whole range of practical tools to promote your e-learning in your organization.

Promotion means getting the word out to prospects and consumers. The objective is to inform, persuade, or remind consumers about a product's attributes and availability (Clemente, 1992). Direct promotion includes personal selling, meetings, in-person demonstrations, direct mail, direct email, and telemarketing. Indirect promotion involves publicity, newsletters, advertising, contests, and sales promotions.

How Much to Invest

How much should you invest in promotion? Think of it this way: If 20 percent of your people are not participating in a $2 million e-learning effort because they didn't know about it or weren't convinced it was for them, you're leaving at least $400,000 on the table.

But, that's looking at it from a cost basis. You don't go to the trouble of developing e-learning just to break even. You're expecting a payback several times the amount you're investing. So maybe you're leaving $1 million in potential benefits on the table. Recognizing that real life is never this simple, wouldn't it be worth $100,000 to put the full-court press on would-be non-participants in the form of publicity, email, hoopla, and a good sales pitch?

Many companies take a half-hearted approach, leaving it to memos and managers to spread the word. If your goal is to increase corporate profits, a dollar spent on publicity that brings more learners into the fold is just as well spent as a dollar invested in instructional design or computer hardware.

Timing Your E-Learning Launch

Launching a new program is easy; maintaining momentum is hard. Many companies make the mistake of treating e-learning like a new baby in the house. After the big celebration and a kickoff party, companies lose interest after unrealistic expectations go unmet. The result of this all-too-familiar cycle is that future learners write off all e-learning as a flash in the pan. It is a better idea to view e-learning as a business process with sustainable value and save the party for when excitement wanes.

COMMUNICATING YOUR MESSAGE

A good marketer uses a variety of media to convey the message to consumers.

Convene the group that will be responsible for communicating with learners for a brainstorming session. Ask the group to brainstorm ideas for communicating with learners before, during, and after e-learning.

Push and Pull Marketing

A basic issue in marketing strategy is whether you want the customer to come to you or you want to go to the customer. Marketers use the terms *push* or *pull* to describe this dynamic, with *push* meaning you (the seller) going to the customer and *pull* meaning the buyer going to the seller.

For example, Laurie Bennett says that most e-learning at Intel is self-directed. Because people are intrinsically motivated, a primary marketing issue is keeping them informed of what's available. Her group uses the Intel intranet, distribution of articles, and demonstrations for the training manager counsel to publicize learning opportunities. This is archetypal pull.

Making participation in e-learning a prerequisite to receiving a promotion would be heavy-handed push. Typically, people love to buy but hate to be sold. Intrinsic motivation is stronger than imposition. Doing your own thing is more motivating than doing someone else's.

The group will probably generate quite a list of ideas. It may include newsletters, press releases, video interviews, local demonstrations, new-hire orientation, sales meetings, in-house advertisements, brochures, endorsements from graduates, posters, table tents, small group sessions, live talks by managers and executives, voicemail, email, direct mail, contests, and previews of coming attractions.

Remember as you deploy your marketing plan that the primary concern of your learners is "What's in it for me?" and the most important thing to communicate to your organization is "What's in it for us?" Be clear that e-learning is a serious business endeavor and not optional or just entertainment. IBM's Karen Kocher says that of the 50 company e-learning programs introduced over the last few years, every winner introduced e-learning as a serious new business initiative.

Communication Tools and Techniques

You have probably thought of a dozen ways that you can let your organization know that e-learning is coming. This section offers some tools and techniques to help you get the message out. Chapter 8 offers some direct help in creating these marketing vehicles.

Brochures. A brochure summarizes the benefits of your learning programs and how to access them. Because many people judge the quality of everything to follow on whatever they see first, a brochure can have tremendous bearing on the success of your efforts. Distribute widely at meetings, by mail, and via your intranet. You can visit the companion Website (www.InternetTime.com) to see some powerful examples of successful e-learning marketing brochures.

Posters and Giveaways. Visual information and physical reminders are critical to winning and keeping the hearts and minds of key stakeholders. New e-learners are more comfortable receiving information about new training opportunities through printed announcements rather than email.

Use your imagination. Don O'Guin at Pharmacia takes advantage of the fact that everybody has to eat. He uses table tents announcing e-learning in company cafeterias.

Eye-catching posters should be placed in strategic locations throughout the organization. Note that on a poster, which is likely to be found in a hallway or on a cluttered bulletin board, you don't have much time to grab your prospect's attention. Use pithy statements to grab the attention of passers-by. PharmaLearn's promotional materials include lines such as "Graduate to a new degree of learning" and "Learn more . . . achieve more." Then provide a Web address where learners can access the program.

It's not always easy to boil your marketing message down to a couple of short sentences. Abraham Lincoln once wrote a correspondent, "I would have written you a shorter letter, but I did not have the time." In the following chapters, you'll receive some advice on how to identify and describe benefits.

E-Learning Briefing Kits. Face-to-face meetings are an essential part of the communications process because they enable critical two-way communications. To ensure a consistent message is being delivered and an open dialogue created, briefing kits are particularly useful. Both leaders and change agents can use them. A kit is typically composed of stand-alone modules that can be mixed and matched to meet the needs of a particular target audience. Flexibility and consistency are the keys.

A typical briefing kit may include instructions on its use, tips on running a question-and-answer session, frequently asked questions and answers, the business case for the project, the project's link to the corporate strategy, the vision and mission statements, anticipated company and personal benefits, videos, handouts, and so forth.

Newsletters. The written word is a powerful communication tool. If you choose to do a newsletter, it should provide regular updates, stories, and interviews that highlight aspects of the project. You can also include information on other topics such as question-and-answer session schedules, rollout schedules, names and profiles of principal team members, lessons learned, relevant articles, glossary of terms, and so on.

You may well want to send out both paper and electronic versions because one key to successful written communication is ease of access by the intended audience. Obviously, a paper version is more expensive to produce and distribute, but an electronic version does not have the same look and feel, nor can it double as a handout or be posted on bulletin boards.

Another key is authenticity. You do not want your newsletter to become another candidate for the "circular file" or an instant "delete." People are inundated with written communications that they see as untruthful or sugarcoated. Tell people what to expect—both the good and the bad. The closer you can get to articulating what really is on learners' and managers' minds, the more effective your newsletter will be.

Videos. A series of videos can be used to present the project's vision, keep it alive over time, and personalize the benefits for key stakeholders. You can develop specific videos to

- present the business case in everyday words and pictures
- provide the 30,000-foot view and then the 10-foot view
- demonstrate the benefits
- validate the benefits through "person-at-work" interviews.

Be clever about where and when to screen these videos. Think about where stakeholders gather, in what settings they are likely to be relaxed and open to receiving new messages. Think hallways, lunch rooms, meeting rooms, and building lobbies. And, if your network can support it, consider posting it on the company intranet or the project intranet site.

The key here is using this powerful medium wisely. Thirty-second sound bites and commercials—with music and glitz—are excellent for creating buzz and interest, but they rarely generate commitment to action. So, in addition to your commercials and coming-attraction pieces, do some man-on-the-street interviews, some day-in-the-life vignettes, and some minidocumentaries. Think infomercial. Infomercials have been wildly successful because they do more than just create excitement, they also educate.

Demonstrations. No matter how many times you say e-learning, it is still necessary for stakeholders to take a test drive, so to speak. "High tech, high touch" should be your motto. Let your stakeholders touch and experiment in a safe environment—before they have to start using it for real.

Make the e-learning available on the project intranet site, offer to come to departmental meetings, and participate in large company events. The more times your learners can touch the e-learning before it goes live, the better. Let them experience the good—and the bad—for themselves. Take the mystery out of it. You can also use these demonstrations as a venue for learning where the resistance is and what the fears are so you can proactively address them.

Organization-wide Events. Events—everything from town hall meetings to yearly status reports to weekly staff meetings—provide other forums for getting messages out. The real value of these events is using them to demonstrate visible support from key leaders. You want to show both learners and management that respected peers and colleagues as well as influential senior managers are not only on board, but vocal advocates.

Think of these events as plays, and you are the producer. Pay attention to the script (what is going to be said) and to the staging (what is being shown and in what order, who is speaking and in what order). Do a dress rehearsal if at all possible. If you can't, meet with the key presenters to prepare them. But, it's important to do a dry run to be sure that your program will work when the lights go on and the curtain goes up.

JOB AIDS

Remember that just as every e-learner has a different learning style, they need different kinds of job aids. The key is making available the right information in the right medium so it can be accessed as quickly as possible. Job aids are just that: aids. They are not manuals or guides. Successful job aids distill the information down to the bare essentials and use graphics whenever possible.

Get some pads of Post-It notes imprinted with cues for learners. Other possibilities include laminated jobs aids, flip-tents, and folded cards. Do whatever you need to do to make sure all e-learners have the tools for success at their desks, at their fingertips.

Design your job aids so that they make it easy for e-learners to use what they already know. Make sure your job aid also uses terms that learners are already familiar with, even if your new e-learning system uses others.

Most important, think process. Most often, e-learners will turn to a job aid when they want to do something and not just find a definition of a menu or command. Identify key processes and build some of your job aids around them.

> ### Innovative Demonstration Venues
>
> Training process leader Dan Gillis reports that Hershey Foods has had great success with Lunch & Learn sessions. Thirty or so people get together for an extended lunch break (an hour instead of 45 minutes) for e-learning show and tell, an introduction, and testimonials. Buzz from these sessions becomes contagious. Hershey also makes this e-learning pitch and introduction available as an agenda item for department meetings.
>
> To drum up business for its e-learning programs, NCR University conducts open houses (called open days in the United Kingdom). These events combine demonstrations, refreshments, receptions, and contests to draw up to 80 percent of the employees in a given location to look at NCRU's new offerings. Usage inevitably skyrockets following each open house. The more remote the office, the higher the level of participation in open houses.

And, finally, build upon existing materials whenever you can. Look for examples of often-used job aids that currently work in your organization and model yours after them.

TIPS

Here are some marketing tips that you should keep in mind as you work through your e-learning launch strategy:

- *Communication channels:* Never assume that everyone receives messages the same way you do.

- *Just enough:* When inviting people to participate in e-learning, keep in mind that you don't have to tell the whole story. A short, crisp note can pack more punch that pages of course descriptions. Less is more.
- *Get blogged:* Blogs (Weblogs) are frequently updated Websites of personal ideas, thoughts, musings, news, and information. These sites are informal, rapid-fire, and they have attitude. Macromedia just set up five blogs for sharing information with customers. Important items pass through the developer community at "blog speed," often propagating around the globe in a matter of hours.
- *Test, test, test:* Direct mail/email are satisfying because it's easy to track results. When you are ready to make a major announcement, test your invitation on a few dozen people first. Gauge their reactions. Merely changing the subject line of an email or the first paragraph of a direct-mail letter can double its effectiveness.
- *Testimonials:* If learners' colleagues extol the greatness of e-learning, you will probably have much more interest in your program. You can videotape these and play them over the intranet, or you can publish written testimonials. Create a tape loop of testimonials, and play it during conferences and sales meetings.

> ## Using People as Your Marketing Agents
>
> The human touch can be the cornerstone for a successful e-learning launch. Call upon your change agents to be "superusers." Make them the best resource when your e-learners have trouble. They may be able to help support hotlines or work on quick-response teams.
>
> Malcolm Gladwell (2000) talks about social mavens who have the ear of not the average 30 contacts but more like 500. Find these personally networked individuals and treat them to preview courseware. Solicit their testimonials for your e-learning.
>
> Some organizations provide a senior manager or a leader who learns with the troops. Your new e-learners want to see their leaders leading. You might also consider recruiting an in-house salesperson. In addition to presenting the product face-to-face, the e-learning salesperson can make service calls, act as a high-level help desk, and investigate needs.

MEASURING SUCCESS

What gets measured gets done. Garner stakeholder buy-in before the e-learning is implemented. After-the-fact measures are akin to the cartoon that shows Charlie Brown drawing the target around the arrow that's already embedded in the tree.

Involving stakeholders is vital because they own the only yardstick that matters. Trainers have traditionally measured such factors as participation rate,

---

Stimulating Buy-In

Stu Tanquist, president of Express Learning, tells of a client who needed to increase utilization of an e-learning program, which was mandatory to meet government regulations. Despite the organization's best efforts to increase understanding, communicate benefits, and promote accountability, e-learning participation suffered due to a lack of buy-in from all levels of the organization.

In partnership with senior management, quarterly expectations were established, and reports were designed to illustrate completion rates by unit, manager, and senior manager. The data was grouped to provide a side-by-side comparison within the management groups and to highlight groups that were not meeting expectations. For example, a manager could view the manager comparison report to see how he or she ranked in relation to the other managers. Within that manager's grouping, the report clearly communicated which areas of responsibility were falling below expectations. The different reports were respectively distributed to the units, managers, and senior managers, including the CEO, on a quarterly basis.

This approach created both internal competition and accountability. Priorities shifted as employees, supervisors, and managers strove to improve their rankings to beat the competition and to meet the increasing expectations of their superiors. As a result, the entire organization finished the year with a 94 percent completion rate.

---

successful completions, test scores, and learner evaluations. Line managers have no interest in these things. They care only about business metrics.

To get management's support and attention, use a balanced scorecard approach, describing accomplishments in terms that relate to improving shareholder value, e.g., increased sales 32 percent, boosted customer satisfaction levels 15 percent, prepared salesforce for new launch in three weeks instead of six, improved turn-down rate in call centers 12 percent. William Horton (2001) provides some clear measures and evaluation methods in another book in this series, *Evaluating E-Learning.*

What if there are no numbers available? Use whatever your sponsor designates as measures for gauging success. Worried that there's no absolute "proof" of the impact of e-learning? That's hardly unique to e-learning. Most business decisions are made under conditions of uncertainty. This is business management, not a science experiment.

Your Turn

This chapter has given you some tools and techniques to launch your e-learning effort. Before going to the next chapter where you will get some advice for actually creating some of the material discussed in this chapter, answer the questions posed in worksheet 7-1 to make sure you have the concepts and techniques down cold.

Worksheet 7-1. Creating your promotional package.

1. Make a list of the communication tools and tactics you plan to use. Identify the messages and audiences.

Communication Tool	Message	Audience
1.		
2.		
3.		
4.		

2. What aspects of your e-learning reflect longer-term thinking and building lifelong relationships?

3. What should you include in communications with learners? You'll remember to focus on your target segments and be true to your brand identity.

8

Practical Advice for the E-Learning Marketer

For want of a persuasive announcement, many learning initiatives have foundered. When you have invested tens or even hundreds of thousands of dollars in e-learning, it pays to refine the words you use to entice people to participate. Until you've written and rewritten a direct mail or email invitation at least five times, you haven't tried very hard.

In this chapter, you will learn how to

- write persuasive, compelling advertising copy
- ignite buzz
- create direct mail and direct email
- sell your e-learning ideas.

WRITING EFFECTIVE ADVERTISING COPY

It is notoriously difficult to measure the impact of a Superbowl commercial or a billboard, but for direct mail it's ridiculously easy. Fifty years of writing direct mail have enabled marketers to measure the effectiveness of tens of thousands of campaigns. To a direct marketer, every ad is an opportunity to experiment. Why run one version of an ad when you can run two and learn more about what makes some ads work and others fail?

Some ads are 20 times more effective than others that look very similar. The successful ads follow these principles:

- What you say is more important than how you say it.
- The headline (the subject if it's email) is the most important element in most advertisements.

- The most effective headlines appeal to the reader's self-interest or give news.
- Long headlines that say something are more effective than short headlines that say nothing.
- Specifics are more believable than generalities.
- Long copy sells more that short copy (Ogilvy, 1974).

The most persuasive words in our culture are *you, money, save, new, results, health, easy, safety, love, discovery, proven,* and *guarantee.* Use them. Try your hand at writing a sentence that uses half a dozen of these words, something like this: "You'll soon discover that our easy-to-use, new Learning Connection will save you time and produce results." You get the idea.

School taught many of us a stilted, artificial style of writing. Better you should write what you feel. You're not being graded. The important thing is to get your message across. Here are some hints from author and teacher Oakley Hall, the general director of a summer program for talented, upcoming novelists:

- Use strong verbs.
- Give details.
- Remember that a specific always beats an abstraction.
- Describe people and places in terms of motion.
- Look for likenesses, parallels, contrasts, antitheses, and reversals.
- In the second draft, start deleting adverbs.
- Borrow widely, steal wisely.
- Say what you need to say, and say no more. Follow the advice of Gustave Flaubert: "Whenever you can shorten a sentence, do. And one always can. The best sentence? The shortest."

How to Ignite Buzz

Word of mouth is a powerful marketing tool. Emanuel Rosen (2000) reports that two-thirds of people buying Palm organizers heard about them from another person. You should use this powerful word-of-mouth phenomenon to market e-learning. Here are some important points on buzz:

- Seed your messages at strategic points in the informal communication network. Give the word and maybe a sample to the natural talkers in the organization—the people who command respect and have large networks. Host sneak previews for influential officials
- Don't roll out the e-learning all at once, or else you don't give the buzz a chance to circulate.

- Roll out e-learning to groups most likely to be enthusiastic about it, and give them a chance to spread the word.
- Stories travel the grapevine rapidly. Describe what's happening among the e-learners as personal vignettes and drip-feed them into the organizational gossip chain.

Here is some further advice from Emanuel Rosen about generating effective buzz:

- Keep it simple. Short, straightforward messages based on current beliefs have a better chance of replicating themselves.
- Tell what's new. Fluff doesn't travel well in the networks.
- Don't make claims you can't support. Learning is not always easy.
- Ask learners to tell you what's special.
- Start measuring buzz. Ask learners what they'd heard in advance of their e-learning.
- Listen to the buzz. Keep your ear to the ground and your eyes on the email.

Create Direct Mail and Email

Getting your reader's attention is your first task as a copywriter for your e-learning project. The next challenge is to put your idea across and do it in a way that appeals to the six prime motives of human action: love, gain, duty, pride, self-indulgence, and self-preservation.

You may not think that an e-learning course carries this much weight, but it does. You are asking for time and attention from the learner.

Keep in mind the building blocks of good copy:

- the opening, which gets the readers' attention by fitting in with their train of thought and establishes a point of contact with their interests, thus exciting curiosity and prompting them to read further
- the descriptions, which picture your proposition

Less Email Is More

Email has worked best at Procter & Gamble for recruiting people for learning. Rather than mail-blasting every employee, the organization selectively targets its emailings. Recently they emailed only associate directors in the United States; another time it was only a certain level of management, no administrative or tech people. Throughout P&G, email must be approved if it is being sent to a distribution list rather than to a handful of individuals. Managers only receive a couple of emails a day from within all of P&G.

Other companies stand in stark contrast. Some send each employee a thousand internal emails each year inviting them to training events; that's five invitations a day! No wonder those emails get scant response.

■ the motive or reason why, which creates a longing in the reader's mind by describing not your proposition but what it will do for him or her: the comfort, the pleasure, the profit he or she will derive from it

■ the proof of guarantee that establishes confidence

■ the snapper or penalty, which gets immediate action by holding over your reader's head the money or prestige or opportunity that will be lost if the reader does not act at once

■ the closing, which tells the reader just what to do and how to do it, and makes it easy for him or her to act at once.

You will find posted on the companion Website (www.InternetTime.com) some examples of effective e-mail and copy.

How to Sell E-Learning

If you want consumers to buy your product, at some point you are going to have to do a sales job. Successful selling is a matter of perseverance and attitude. More important, selling e-learning is a matter of overcoming obstacles.

Overcoming Obstacles

Resistance to e-learning centers around six obstacles. The learner

1. reports an unfavorable first-time experience
2. dislikes change
3. thinks e-learning is not as good as a live workshop
4. does not like isolation
5. prefers off-site workshops
6. resents the added workload.

Senior executives from a variety of industries describe these seven barriers to implementing e-learning:

1. time employees have available for training
2. cost versus value
3. difficulty of measuring results
4. quality of learning content
5. perceived difficulty of using such a system
6. technology infrastructure
7. internal resistance to using technology instead of face-to-face learning.

So, what obstacles are you likely to encounter and how can you overcome them?

Almost certainly you don't have an e-learning salesforce, but some obstacles are only overcome by selling someone your ideas. Successful selling is a matter of perseverance and attitude. "It comes down to caring about your customers. My purpose: I help people get the feelings they want—soon" (Wilson & Johnson, 1986). In essence, people don't buy services, products, or ideas. They buy how they imagine using them will make them feel. Frankly, if you run the numbers you might find that hiring a few inside e-learning account executives has a higher payback than broadening the curriculum.

Don't try to do too much too soon. Selling is incremental. Big sales are built on little sales. Psychologist Robert Ornstein writes that if people are asked to contribute to a good cause, 20 percent of them will. That may seem like a small number, but you can build on it. Consider that most people would balk at planting a sign that is 6 feet by 8 feet promoting the beauty of California in their front yards. Yet, if you first convince them to put a 3-by-5-inch card in their front window, a couple of weeks later, most of them will agree to put up the large sign.

What's the point of this story? Kick things off with something short and easy to complete. Build upon your small successes to create big successes.

Here are some overarching conclusions that will make your sell job easier. E-learners need

- ▓ *Collaboration:* Technology should provide access to content and other people.
- ▓ *Integration:* Learning solutions must be based on proven principles of adult learning that leverage multiple delivery media.
- ▓ *Relevance:* Embedding learning into work processes results in significant and sustainable performance improvement for both the individual and the business.
- ▓ *Fundamentals:* In their haste to adopt e-learning, some companies lose sight of the fundamental principles of adult learning and focus more on the technology involved. Technology, or any other delivery medium, is a means to deliver effective learning and not an end in itself.

Selling: How It's Done at Aspect

The Learning Center at Aspect Communications knows that it has to sell employees on the rewards of training. When Aspect rolled out a new approach to learning, the Learning Center staff held demonstration parties at facilities around the globe for all employees to learn about the new e-learning offerings. Daylong affairs, the demonstration parties featured food, drink, and prizes. People could drop by for a look at what was new or attend a group event. About half of Aspect's employees took part.

In a similar vein, the Learning Center conducted a sales resources fair at the firm's global sales meeting, and the sales training organization regularly holds contests of the month to promote new initiatives.

Packaging E-Learning

People do judge a book by its cover. Keep the quality of your packaging consistent and pleasing. The packaging for your e-learning might be a CD jewel box, a log-in screen, or companion materials. Your packaging choices influence the success of your e-learning initiative.

The Learning Center at Aspect Communications has all the attributes of an in-house brand. Graphic treatment is consistent across posters, log-in screens, catalogs, fliers, signage, and even beverage holders (figure 8-1).

Figure 8-1. The Learning Center's e-learning packaging.

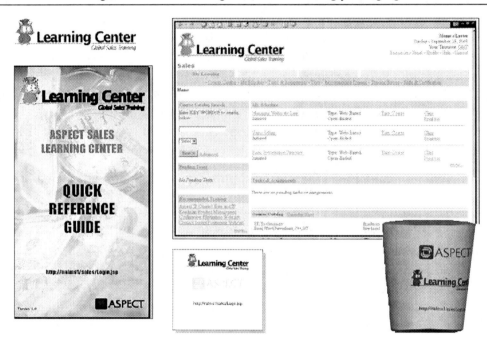

YOUR TURN

Successful selling, as you likely know, is a matter of perseverance and attitude. If you are able to anticipate obstacles, it will be easier to overcome them, or better, avoid them entirely. Try your hand at worksheet 8-1, remembering that the keys to conquering e-learning obstacles are collaboration, integration, relevance, and the fundamentals.

Worksheet 8-1. Overcoming obstacles to e-learning.

Place a checkmark next to obstacles that you foresee could affect your e-learning. Then, propose some ways to avoid or overcome the potential obstacles.

Obstacle	Potential Obstacle? ✓	Possible Solution(s)
Learner-Related Obstacles		
Reports an unfavorable first-time experience		
Dislikes change		
Thinks e-learning is not as good as a live workshop		
Does not like isolation		
Prefers off-site workshops		
Resents the added workload		
Organizational Obstacles		
Time employees have available for training		
Cost versus value		
Difficulty of measuring results		
Quality of learning content		
Perceived difficulty of using such a system		
Technology infrastructure		
Internal resistance to using technology instead of face-to-face learning		

9

Sustaining Your Marketing and Implementation Efforts

It's one thing to launch a successful marketing campaign and implementation program. That, in some ways, is the easy part. Renewing the inaugural excitement, keeping spirits up, and sustaining success is what's tough. From a marketing perspective, sustaining success requires exceeding learners' expectations. Instructors, mentors, designers, developers, and anyone else administering e-learning must have the spirit and desire to put long-term learner/customer benefits above all else. From a change management perspective, sustaining success requires that the organization move toward institutionalizing e-learning, making it a part of the very fabric of everyday work life.

KEEPING YOUR E-LEARNING CUSTOMERS

If you want to keep your e-learning customers, take some lessons from the retailing industry. Few businesses are as unforgiving as retailing. Retailers invest massive amounts of money in stores, information systems, advertising, catalogs, and payroll to sell products to a fickle public. A retailer can be first class in every other aspect, but if it fails at customer service, the company could fail.

If you are interested in some service pointers that you might use in your e-learning marketing and implementation plan, heed the advice of Leonard Berry (1999):

- Value and price do not mean the same thing to customers.
- When senior managers and employees share the same guiding principles and the same organizational values, providing excellent service is easier.
- Value-driven leaders mobilize emotional and spiritual resources to drive superior service.

- Leaders need a core strategy that galvanizes the human spirit and transforms potential into performance.
- Active listening reveals opportunities for improving service.
- Staying customer-focused helps organizations control their destiny.
- Learning is a journey, not a destination.
- Organizational size does not guarantee success.
- Winning the hearts of employees creates a business where human beings create value for human beings.

As the leader of an e-learning effort or someone who is expected to know how to make e-learning succeed, you can connect Berry's principles to your e-learning effort.

HOW HAPPY ARE YOUR E-LEARNING CUSTOMERS?

Learners seek value that exceeds expectations. Keep your fingers on the learners' pulse if you expect to meet this challenge. An old customer service rule of thumb holds that one customer in five is dissatisfied, but only one in 20 lodges a formal complaint. Here are some ideas that you can put into place to get this valuable information:

- *Complaint and suggestion systems:* These systems can be good sources of ideas for improvement. You will collect better feedback if you go beyond the typical smile sheet dashed off in the last two minutes of a learning experience.
- *Customer satisfaction surveys:* Telephone calls elicit better information than written questionnaires. Sometimes you can make a few calls to get anecdotal information from your learners and use this as a basis to create a more elaborate survey.
- *Mystery shopping:* Banks and restaurants hire people to sample their services and food and report back on the experience. You can apply the same technique to your e-learning marketing and implementation program.
- *Lost customer analysis:* Take a look at all those who do not finish the course and find out why. Often when you stop using a service or stop buying a product, the product or service owner wants to know why.

MAKING LEARNING FUN

Contemporary culture often mocks school as a prison or madhouse. Even if these comments come in the form of jokes, training and learning programs sometimes get a bum rap in the minds of learners, even those who are highly motivated adult learners. Malcolm Knowles (1990) claims that adults learn best when they feel in control, when they are able to learn by doing, and when they see the reason for the learning. Few in the business world have read Knowles' book, but applying some of the principles in this book could make a big difference in any organization's understanding of learning.

RESPECT THE LEARNER

Learners' complaints and questions may not always reflect actuality, but you can't ignore them if you are to keep your e-learning effort alive and well. Retail marketing and e-learning both have "low barriers to exit." It's always easy for a customer to bail out by either walking out the door or clicking the exit button. Leonard Berry (1999) offers excellent advice for earning and keeping the customer's respect. Many of his ideas translate to e-learning, for example:

- Do you stand behind what you sell? Is your e-learning easy to use and access? Do you and your team fix problems as they occur? Does the learner feel that you and your team have a sense of urgency to solve the learner's problems? Do you guarantee your service?
- Do you emphasize the importance of keeping promises? Are your commitments to learners given high priority?
- Do you value your learners' time? Do you anticipate periods of peak demand for your offerings and maintain the infrastructure necessary to minimize downtime and delayed access? Do you maintain an adequate staff for the help desk?
- Are your systems convenient and efficient for learners to use? Do you orient new team members about your commitment to learners?
- Do you communicate with learners respectfully? Are your directions informative and helpful? Are your statements clear and understandable? Do you respond to learner queries promptly and courteously? Do you monitor your email regularly to ensure fast responses?
- Do you respect all learners? Have you taken any special precautions to ensure accessibility of your e-learning programs to everyone in the organization?
- Do you thank learners for their participation? Do your customers feel appreciated?

CELEBRATING YOUR E-LEARNING SUCCESS

The objective of your e-learning efforts is to create long-term relationships with your learners. This is the key to sustaining your e-learning efforts.

Organizations sometimes reward "graduating" or "honors" learners with cash awards, prizes, raffle tickets, holiday trips, or merchandise. Although this technique may have some benefit, don't count on giveaways to keep your learners interested.

Overall, the carrot-and-stick approach is not optimal. Your goal should be to get your learners participating in the e-learning that is necessary to increase their performance. If you provide worthwhile services, your customers will come. An employee who is not learning is by definition stagnant. Tying learning accomplishment to performance review provides incentive for keeping up.

LET THE LEARNERS PARTICIPATE

By giving learners a voice in shaping the e-learning system, you foster participation, generate excitement, and keep the program on target. If learners participate in improving your e-learning programs, their commitment to and enthusiasm for your programs grows and spreads to others in the organization. Here are a few ways that you can ensure this participation:

- *Help desk:* Aspect Communications provides a Help Desk to answer questions from its salesforce. Every incoming question is logged, and the logs are analyzed to identify issues that need to be improved in training. This learner feedback is used to improve existing programs and serve as the impetus to create new programs.
- *Learner councils:* Learner councils study and suggest ways to move your e-learning initiatives ahead.
- *Evaluation publicity:* Consider making learner evaluations public. Demonstrate how future modifications and enhancements build upon these evaluations. Learners like to see that their input matters.
- *Demonstrations of caring and commitment:* Learners need to know that you (and your organization) care about their learning. You can do this by providing guidance on future learning and keeping them informed about future learning opportunities. Personal service is also important. Go out of your way to keep e-learners' interest at heart.

MAINTAINING YOUR E-LEARNING EDGE

The e-learning group in a corporate environment often grapples with the same pressures as any stand-up trainer: long hours, unrealistic deadlines, technical glitches, and multiple demands. The leader of such a group will do well to build a professional community incorporating the following:

■ reflective dialogue
■ unity of purpose
■ collective focus on learning
■ collaboration and norms of sharing
■ openness to improvement
■ trust and respect
■ renewal of community
■ supportive and knowledgeable leadership.

Network with others in your field, both within your company and at other organizations. Share your discoveries with others. Reflect on the longer-term impact of your work. Team up with others to improve the learning environment. Become active in organizations such as ASTD, International Society for Performance Improvement, and the e-Learning Guild, both locally and on a national level. Participate in local organizations such as the e-Learning Forum in the Bay Area. Attend conferences. Don't be a naysayer—and don't let others lose the faith. When faced with adversity, ask yourself, "What can I learn from this?" Respect others and they will respect you.

Building a Learning Community

Building community extends the learning process. Participants in IBM's Basic Blue managerial training program—a blended learning experience—are assigned to learning groups of 10 to 20. They study together, learn together, and solve problems together. Many of the groups continue to network and learn from one another after the completion of the formal program.

Many organizations pair novice learners with experienced learners. The novice learns the ropes from the old hand. The old hand reinforces his or her own knowledge by instructing the novice. Both learn more than either would have on their own.

Making E-Learning Part of Your Culture

Your initial implementation is just the first step in the process to make e-learning truly part of your organization's culture. Be patient. It's going to take a while. After all, changing a culture is typically a long and difficult process. Unless your organization is in the midst of some crisis or a "burning platform for change," expect the timeframe to be years and not months.

And, remember always that organizations don't change, people do. So, you need to direct your efforts to making e-learning a regular part of every employee's work life, and making it second nature to learners, managers, and executive alike.

CONTINUE TO COMMUNICATE

Communication must never stop. At this stage, it is important to communicate results. What has happened to date? How does this compare with what was expected? What are e-learners, trainers, managers, and all the stakeholders saying about their initial experience—both the good and the bad?

Obviously, hearing positive messages reinforces the new performance. But, being truthful will build lasting trust with you, the learners, and the stakeholders. After all, it's unlikely that your implementation proceeded without a hitch and that everyone is happy. And, you know what? Everyone knows that. So, using the various communication channels and tools at your disposal, tell your story.

Use one-on-one meetings to brief your stakeholders and influencers and secure their ongoing support. Focus on both tangible and intangible business results. Talk about the things that are easy to measure (how much money was saved, how many more people were trained, how much time was saved). But, also talk about those that potentially have a greater impact but are harder to quantify (time to performance, value of customer retention due to improved service quality). Focus on the role of e-learning as a business strategy to improve the top and bottom line rather than its value as a training project or cost-saving measure. Use mass-media channels to maintain the buzz and build momentum for the next phases with your e-learners and their managers.

Resistance is to be expected. Everyone resists change initially, especially if they feel a loss of control. No one likes to "be changed" or feel pushed. So, simply repeating the same phrases to try to convince or persuade them only means they will dig in their heels deeper. It's critical now to increase your pull marketing strategies.

The best way to increase your "pull" is to increasingly personalize the communications in these areas:

- why e-learning is better than other alternatives
- what is similar in e-learning to what they already know
- how easy e-learning is to use
- how easy it is to just try it
- where they can see e-learning in action
- what their peers are saying about e-learning.

Communicating these messages over and over again in a personal way will move the innovators to early adopters and then to the early majority. Remember, it's only necessary to secure the commitment of 5 percent of the learners and managers to imbed e-learning in your organization and create the pull necessary to reach the 20 percent "critical mass" necessary to make it unstoppable. (Refer back to Everett Rogers's diffusion of innovation model in chapter 2.)

Use your change agents to personalize the messages to as many people as possible. Highlight the positive, both in terms of hard results (measurable savings or increases) and soft results (personal testimonials). Use what didn't work as a springboard for bringing the resisters on board to inspire improvements. After all, those who are the resisters have the courage and the conviction to articulate their concerns and present a challenge. You want them on your side. Surprisingly, if they feel you have listened to them it's easy to redirect their resistance to active support.

PULL THE RIGHT LEVERS

Because organizations are systems (chapter 3), institutionalizing e-learning requires that you pull a number of levers. Aligning your human resource systems—particularly your performance management and compensation systems—is the one of first levers to pull to move toward embedding e-learning into your corporate culture. Why compensation is a lever goes without saying; people do what they are paid to do. Although it's not typical to pay learners to take courses, there are other ways to financially reward learners, however. For example, your e-learning system can make it possible for employees to manage their own career development and prepare themselves for promotions and pay increases.

Performance management systems shape the working lives and careers of your e-learners and, therefore, are also strong levers to change behaviors. For example, at IBM, participation in e-learning is a prerequisite to additional management training. And, at Novartis Pharma, the e-learning platform is the only means by which the salesforce and its supervisors can manage their development and certifications.

> ### Share the Glory
>
> Through her leadership, Kara Underwood at Aspect Communications ensures that all members of her team receive credit for their accomplishments. Together, they have designed and implemented an award-winning strategic sales training program that drastically reduced ramp time for new hires. All too often, the boss takes all the credit for such accomplishments, but not Kara. She gets her team members into the limelight, too.

There are also formal and informal reward and recognition subsystems that are key to influencing behaviors. For example, you can acknowledge your e-learners—and their managers—in company publications and make sure they are mentioned at company events. You can also point out management situations in which resistance to e-learning has cost the individual and the organization. The bottom line here is that social approval and disapproval are powerful levers for changing behavior.

It goes without saying that people do what they perceive as being in their best interest. If e-learning is a means to an end, then it becomes an integral part of the corporate culture.

Another powerful lever for change is alignment of your e-learning efforts with critical organizational initiatives and business goals. It is often said that an organization can't save its way to success. Therefore, positioning e-learning only as a cost-savings strategy is short-sighted. The same is true with positioning e-learning as a training project. Instead, find the business initiatives that already have the support of senior management and show how e-learning can enable their success.

For example, if your organization is embarked on some type of organizational change (for example, rolling out a new CRM or ERP, redesigning business processes, business consolidation or expansion), you can develop and communicate a business case to show how e-learning will shorten the time necessary for all employees affected by the change to become optimal performers—while saving money—based on the results of your implementation to date. You now have hard data, facts, and figures. You also have soft data, opinions, and impressions. Share them. It's good business.

Over time, there will no longer be the need to build the business case for each new initiative because e-learning will be institutionalized, and e-learning will be integral to how your organization does business, day to day and year to year.

Your Turn

Using the concepts discussed in this chapter, write a three-page strategy for keeping e-learning alive at your company. Often treated as an afterthought, it's the sustainment strategy that brings many e-learning programs to their knees after a successful start. Address how you plan to keep your customers in the race, earn the continuing support of your stakeholders, and institutionalize a learning culture. Worksheet 9-1 poses questions to guide your answers.

Worksheet 9-1. Create a strategy for sustaining your e-learning.

We will keep our customers over time:

- How will you provide feedback to learners and their bosses?
- How will you handle complaints?
- How will you assess customer satisfaction?
- How will you stay customer-focused?
- How will you show your customers that you respect them?
- Do you plan to use "mystery learners"?
- How will learners be able to co-create future learning events?
- Are you setting up a learner council?
- Are experienced employees to mentor new employees?
- How will you support the development of communities of practice?

We will keep our stakeholders engaged:

- How frequently will you provide progress reports?
- What will be in those reports?
- How will you identify or solicit new challenges?
- How will you monitor satisfaction?
- How will stakeholders request improvements or additions?
- Are you setting up a board of advisors or a steering committee?

We will institutionalize e-learning in our corporate culture:

- Is professional development of one's direct reports in managers' job descriptions?
- Have supervisors themselves learned to support and reinforce their subordinates' learning?
- What HR systems need to be changed?
- What performance management systems need to be changed?
- What formal and informal rewards and recognition systems will you leverage?
- What organizational initiatives will you seek to become part of?

10

Taking Action

By the time you reach the conclusion of this chapter, you will have completed an e-learning implementation action plan for your organization and will be ready to put it into practice.

A PLACE IN HISTORY

You may not have realized it, but you are a pioneer at the vanguard of the second century of change that's sweeping business and training. In the beginning of the 20th century, goods were scarce. Businesses were known by what they made. A business was a shoe company or a car company or a training company. Efficiency was the road to success. You prospered by making shoes better than the competition did. If your company sold more, you achieved economies of scale, and you sold more still. Time-and-motion experts lauded the "one best way" to do things. This pursuit of efficiency became known as the manufacturing mindset. It was the road to profit. Those were the days when the world moved slowly. Little changed quickly.

In mid-century, our current notion of corporate training was refined out of pure necessity. At the beginning of World War II, the United States had no standing army. To prepare several million troops for battle, the military called upon the lessons of Henry Ford and other great pioneers of the industrial revolution. They replaced apprenticeship with courses, more or less inventing training films and instructional design along the way. Although accelerated by World War II, the pace of change was manageable. Think radio and the promise of an automobile in every driveway. ASTD was formed in 1944.

After the war, big corporations appeared, their hierarchies reflecting the command-and-control structure of the military. Corporate management became a discipline practiced by corporate officers. New managers applied the manufacturing mindset to training, counting "butts in seats" and looking for immediate returns. Given a steady and predictable rate of change, strategic planning became critical to corporate success. After all, it was believed that you could clearly see what the future would hold three to five years down the line.

Entering the 21st century, goods were abundant. Business has realized with the help of management guru Peter Drucker that customers don't buy things, they buy value, and value is in the mind of the beholder. Instead of joining the time-and-motion experts looking for improvements inside the organization, winning companies began looking at things from their customers' perspective, from outside the organization. This customer-centric approach has become known as the marketing mindset.

As the pace of change continued to accelerate, the flexibility inherent in the marketing mindset became one of the keys to corporate survival. The ability not only to manage change adeptly but to lead it has become the other. Time is of the essence. Companies that don't manage change falter, and those that don't change die.

This book brings both the marketing mindset and the change management perspective to corporate learning. Learning is to training as is marketing to selling as managing change is to directing it. Selling involves convincing the customer to buy what you have. Marketing means understanding what customers value in order to have it to offer. Change management means understanding the process that people and an organization goes through to successfully embrace something new.

Now you can complete the final steps to put the marketing mindset and change management perspective into action.

Implementation Soup

Learning to navigate implementation soup is like learning to drive a vehicle with a stick shift. At first you fear you'll never get the hang of it. Distractions come from all directions. You marvel at people who can run through the gears effortlessly. Yet a few weeks later, you're shifting smoothly, and in time the whole process becomes second nature.

So it is with implementing e-learning. At first it seems to be made up of myriad, unrelated ingredients that will never come together. It's tough to tell when you're going far enough and when you're going too far. You marvel at people who see things clearly. But, as you go through the regimen of putting customer relationships before all else, of being alert to change, of crafting well-designed messages, and of following sound business practice, things become clear. Some time later, you're acting like a combination change management/marketing professional. The whole process becomes second nature.

Your E-Learning Implementation Source Document

It's time to shift from theory to practice. You will be integrating your findings, your analysis, your planning, and your tactics into a unified plan.

To begin, put all of the material you developed while working your way through *Implementing E-Learning* into a single large Microsoft Word file. This will be your raw material for assembling the action plan you'll share with others. Name it "Source Document." You may create the source document from scratch, using the model in the Your Turn section that follows or by downloading the source document template from www.InternetTime.com. Do this now.

You will probably want to double-check the tips discussion at www .InternetTime.com for last-minute pointers, updates, and examples. (By the way, please submit samples of what works for you to share with others faced with the same task.)

Every organization has its traditions and rules about how information is disseminated. The template provides some boilerplate text and questions to answer. If your organization demands more formality, depth, analysis, cost/benefit, or project payback, by all means add it. Or, delete it if less is called for. Use the source document template as a guide, but temper its instructions based on your knowledge of what works best at your organization.

Refining Your Action Plan

Reflect on the findings and plans in your source document. Get other people's perspectives. Discuss your findings with peers and innovators amongst key stakeholder groups. Bounce ideas off people you meet at conferences and local ASTD chapter meetings. If you find areas you didn't do justice to in the course of reading this book, use this opportunity to go back and do them right.

Read through your source document. Is everything consistent? Expect to make changes; dealing with the whole will generate new perspectives. You're switching from chopping down trees to managing a forest. Is this the best you can do? Where are the holes? What's the riskiest aspect of your evolving plan?

Implementing e-learning is always an iterative, try-it/fix-it process, but you should start off on the most solid footing possible. It's at least a dozen times easier to change course in the planning stage, before beginning your launch, than during it.

Satisfied? Then comb through your source document, summarizing your findings and pulling out powerful one-liners and examples. Use these to write your action plan, a one- to three-page memo or half a dozen PowerPoint slides delineating your conclusions. Brevity is beautiful.

Drop anything you cannot take responsibility for. In other words, eliminate all hogwash, hype, and conjecture from your plan. This is a good time to remind yourself that authenticity is one of the keys to effective communication.

Keep in mind that you should not share your source document with all the stakeholders, for to do so would demonstrate your naiveté in business. Your source document is like an unedited movie; it plays much better after being chopped, spliced, and made coherent. Restating the ideas people already know or those that have no impact disrespects your stakeholders' time and intelligence.

PRESENTING YOUR ACTION PLAN

When a stakeholder or other interested party wants in-depth information, present it in person. If you chose to develop your plan in Word, now is the time to create the PowerPoint version. These meetings are great opportunities not only to answer questions and solicit feedback, but also build rapport and find out where you stand. Your presentation may include the topics you've encountered in *Implementing E-learning:*

- elevator pitch
- what you need to do, background
- vision and mission for e-learning
- your organization's culture and change
- your communication plan
- why you're marketing and branding
- research findings and industry analysis
- brand, target markets, positioning
- sustaining and renewal plans
- obstacles expected
- how e-learning—and you—can help.

Don't expect to give precisely this presentation. No one's going to ask for your internal documents. This is new turf. Instead, expect to pick and choose from among these topics based on your audience. Remember to focus on the fact that these plans are for making sure employees and customers get the most out of your e-learning and to ensure your organization can avoid the pitfalls that have tripped up so many companies' e-learning efforts.

Sometimes your best bet is to hand-carry copies of your action plan to stakeholders and walk them through it to confirm that it meshes with their expectations. Sell the plan to skeptics and ask for support from the favorably disposed. Use printouts of the PowerPoint slides if needed to make your point. Once approved, the plan may be posted on the company's intranet, giving responsibility to the entire organization for keeping it on target. Your approach may include some or all or none of these elements. You know your organization. Act accordingly.

Remember what you've just put together—a plan for implementing e-learning from a marketing and change management perspective. This plan complements your other plans, which detail schedules, timing, technology support, and so forth; it does not replace them. Know that by developing and articulating the change and marketing aspects of your e-learning implementation, you're ahead of the 99 percent of organizations where these plans are jotted on the back of an envelope, if made at all.

JUST DO IT!

Great implementation plans are worthless if they are not, well, implemented. You are equipped now to begin this critical next phase of your work. Share your plans, refine them, evangelize them, and then put them into action.

Good luck. Please share your results with us at www.InternetTime.com.

YOUR TURN

Here it is—your source document template! You can use worksheet 10-1, or you may download the template as a Word file from the companion Website (www.InternetTime.com). Keep in mind that you will need to modify the boilerplate text so that it is appropriate for your organization.

Worksheet 10-1. Input for your e-learning implementation action plan.

Consolidate the information you developed in the previous chapters into this worksheet. You can download the most up-to-date version from www.InternetTime.com. The online worksheet is in Word, so you can cut and paste information from various sources.

After you have everything you need in one place, go back through the worksheet, making things consistent, refining your plans, adding details as appropriate, and deleting things that don't make a difference. Add a schedule of events. What remains is your E-learning Implementation Action Plan. Congratulations.

Subject: How We Plan to Make Our E-Learning a Success

This memo summarizes why we are implementing e-learning and how it will benefit our organization. We will share how we plan to integrate e-learning into our corporate culture and operations, where we expect—or need—organizational support, and how the company will gain from the e-learning imitative. We will share the description we propose for e-learning and a summary of our communications plan.

We have just completed a rigorous analysis of what it will take for our organization to maximize its ROI in e-learning. Specifically, we set about answering these three questions:

1. What can we do to prepare our employees, customers, and partners to get the most from e-learning?

2. How can we improve the odds of success?

3. How do we keep people coming back for more?

In the past, offering individual courses and workshops, we were content to assume that we knew the answers to these questions. These individual courses don't justify market analysis and campaigns. Our e-learning effort does, though, because

- e-learning is an ongoing process, not an event
- e-learning represents large-scale organizational change
- not everyone is on board
- a large investment is at stake
- achieving results is no longer optional
- many people do not understand what e-learning is
- skeptics are critical of its effectiveness.

Our in-house goals are to

- motivate learners, managers, and the entire organization
- win the support of our varied stakeholders
- build an e-learning infrastructure
- achieve lasting results.

In a nutshell, our action plan is to...

Insert your elevator pitch from chapter 6. Briefly describe your proposed brand identity, target markets, and positioning.

Challenges (from chapter 1)

1. What is your gut instinct about the challenges you will face?

2. Take a look at factors within your organization that may help or hinder your implementation. How many good signs do you see and what are they?

3. What are the bad signs you need to watch out for or plan to address?

Business Issues (from chapter 2)

1. The primary business issues involving our e-learning are:

2. Who are your major stakeholders? Owners? Managers? Workers? Partners? Outside customers?

3. How does your proposal support the vision of management?

4. How does this e-learning create value for your stakeholders?

5. What trade-offs are you making?

6. Describe the risk in your proposal and compare it to the rewards.

7. How do you think your customers will feel?

8. How are you applying the 80/20 rule? What high-leverage groups or activities have you chosen?

9. What impact will your initiative have on the bottom line?

(continued on page 122)

**Worksheet 10-1. Source document template
for your e-learning implementation action plan (continued)**

10. How does your e-learning focus on core strategic issues instead of context?

11. Describe the cost-benefit analysis for your proposal.

12. The primary change management issues involving our e-learning are:

13. What leads to the sense of urgency around this project?

14. Who is on your guiding coalition?

15. What corporate changes are you attaching your e-learning wagon to?

16. What short-term wins do you foresee?

17. What stakeholders can you recruit for your coalition?

18. How will you anchor e-learning in your culture?

19. How do you plan to recruit innovators and early adopters?

20. Who are our primary customers? Employees? Salespeople? Customers?

21. What is the clear and compelling promise of your brand?

22. Describe the relationship you seek with your customers.

Organizational Culture and Change (from chapters 3 and 4)

1. We must keep in mind that our organizational culture is:
   [List some characteristics of your culture here.]

2. What artifacts typify your organization's culture?

3. What are the distinct features of your corporate culture?

4. Where do you see your culture on Hofstede's scales?

Equality	◄---------------------------►	Inequality
Individualism	◄---------------------------►	Collectivism
Masculine	◄---------------------------►	Gender equality
Risk-averse	◄---------------------------►	Pro-change
Long-term	◄---------------------------►	In the moment

   And how might this encourage or block e-learning?

5. We are preparing to support our e-learning implementation through leadership. Which organizational leaders are backing our efforts and why?

6. Who are our change agents and why?

7. What will we do to support them?

8. Are the learners prepared for this change?

9. Is our organization prepared for change?

10. Is our technology up to the task?

(continued on page 124)

**Worksheet 10-1. Source document template
for your e-learning implementation action plan (continued)**

11. How will the initiative be governed?

12. Do the skills, knowledge, and abilities exist in our organization to ensure the success of our implementation?

13. What is our vision? [Remember, a vision statement is a picture of what you want the future to look like—what you aspire to become, to achieve, to create.]

14. What is our mission? [Remember, your mission examines the project's purpose and expresses its sense of value. Perhaps most important, a mission inspires people to stand out, and it guides leaders.]

15. What are the audiences we need to reach with our change communication plan?

16. What are the messages these audiences need to hear, and when?

17. What are the communication vehicles and activities we'll use?

18. What will we do increase awareness?

19. What will we do to increase involvement?

20. What will we do to increase commitment?

Market Research (from chapter 5)

1. We have used the following research methods to underpin our market research plan:

    *   To learn about our consumers, the learners, we undertook this research:

    *   To learn about consumer behavior, we undertook this research:

    *   To learn about competitors for consumers' attention, we undertook this research:

    *   To learn about sponsors, we undertook this research:

    *   To learn about our brand image, we undertook this research:

    *   To learn about organizational goals, we undertook this research:

    *   To learn about our industry's environment, we undertook this research:

    *   To learn about the macroeconomic environment, we undertook this research:

    *   To learn about trends in e-learning technology, we undertook this research:

Let's look at each area in turn.

2. *Our consumers:* We've identified and described the target customers for our e-learning.
    The consumers, your customers, are the most important topic of all. Use the 80/20 rule to select the groups with the most likely impact. Then describe each group using a target consumer description form. Two forms are provided below. See figure 5-1 for some examples of how to do this.

Target Customer Description
Identity:
Number:
Location:
Tenure:
Turnover:
New hires:
Learning needs:
Line sponsor:
Bottom-line impact expected:

(continued on page 126)

**Worksheet 10-1. Source document template
for your e-learning implementation action plan (continued)**

Target Customer Description

Identity:

Number:

Location:

Tenure:

Turnover:

New hires:

Learning needs:

Line sponsor:

Bottom-line impact expected:

---

3. *Competitors:* We've identified the major competitors, for the time, of our employees.

   • What or who are your major competitors?

   • What other corporate priorities will you be competing against?

   • What objections do you expect from your customers?

4. *Sponsors:* We've coordinated our plans with many people in the organization.

   • Who are our executive sponsors? What's in it for them?

   • Who are our line management sponsors? What's in it for them?

   • Who are our technical sponsors? What's in it for them?

   • Whom must we rely on for success? What's in it for them?

   • How do we plan to get their backing and support?

5. *Organizational goals:* We know and support what our company is trying to accomplish.

   • What are our organization's overall goals?

   • What is the current mandate from executive management?

   • How does our e-learning initiative relate to its achievement?

6. *Our industry's environment:* In light of the direction in our industry, we've identified trends that will influence our e-learning initiatives.

   • What are the major trends in our industry?

   • Is solution selling replacing point sales?

   • Are customers going for self-service?

   • Is automation changing the flow of work?

   • Is the enterprise becoming more international?

   • Are processes being outsourced or moving overseas?

   • Are competitors introducing new generations of products?

7. *Macroeconomic environment:* We expect that global events will affect our industry and its need for learning.

   • What political, economic, and social changes in the world at large may affect our business?

   • What impact do you expect from increasing workforce diversity? Aging of the workforce? Economic volatility? Declining half-life of knowledge? Faster pace of business? Increased regulation? Globalization? International terrorism? Declining public education standards? Other factors?

   • How do we plan to adapt to the changes deemed relevant to our industry?

8. *Learning technology:* In all likelihood, the next three years will see shifts in e-learning technology, and we need to lay the groundwork for adaptation now as

   • learning and knowledge management converge
   • e-learning becomes a Web service
   • simulation replaces linear subject orientation
   • e-learning and other enterprisewide systems converge
   • content becomes more industry-specific
   • extent of high-quality generic content increases in core areas
   • individualized learning prescriptions are based on competency assessments
   • competency management replaces needs analysis.

If you've shared your findings with others, perhaps via your intranet, describe the confirmation or suggestions you've received from others.

(continued on page 128)

**Worksheet 10-1. Source document template
for your e-learning implementation action plan (continued)**

Your market research could fill an extensive report, but you shouldn't let it. Go back through your findings and eliminate anything that doesn't matter. After all, not every industry trend or competitor is going to make even a ripple in your e-learning pond. Less is more. Pick the two or three most striking findings in each category, and use them to write a terse market research summary.

Marketing Design (from chapter 6)

Effective consumer marketing strategies rest on a foundation of

- a brand that creates a reputation that keeps customers coming back and attracts new customers
- market segmentation that optimizes results by leveraging the most appropriate groups of customers
- a position that places your product in the "sweet spot" in the mind of the customer.

We have used these concepts to develop our e-learning implementation plan:
[Restate your elevator pitch here.]

1. What do we want our organization and services to be known for? What do we promise our customers?

2. What is our functional value proposition to our consumers?

3. What is our emotional value proposition to our consumers?

4. How will our brand identity give meaning to the lives of our customers?

5. Just as a brand identity may reflect a person (personality), it may reflect an organization and its culture. What attributes of your organization might you incorporate into your brand identity?

   With these factors in mind, the brand identity of our e-learning consists of the following elements:

   - brand name:

   - brand symbol or logo:

   - a few core values:

6. What are our target markets and why did we choose them?

7. Which market segments will we focus on?

8. Choose the most relevant pairs of scales to show where our e-learning efforts are starting and where we'd like to take them in the coming 12 to 36 months.

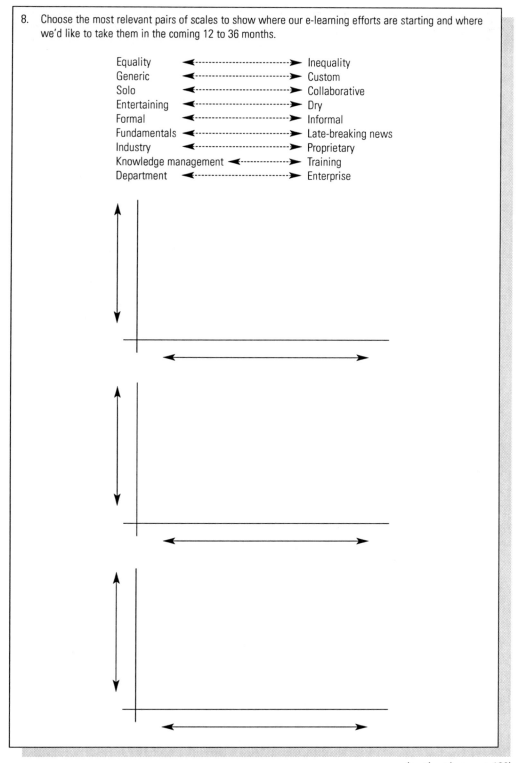

Equality   ⬅------------------------➡   Inequality
Generic   ⬅------------------------➡   Custom
Solo   ⬅------------------------➡   Collaborative
Entertaining   ⬅------------------------➡   Dry
Formal   ⬅------------------------➡   Informal
Fundamentals   ⬅------------------------➡   Late-breaking news
Industry   ⬅------------------------➡   Proprietary
Knowledge management   ⬅--------------➡   Training
Department   ⬅------------------------➡   Enterprise

(continued on page 130)

Launch (from chapters 7 and 8)

Include the materials you developed in chapters 7 and 8, for example: a three-paragraph email announcing the e-learning initiative, a draft brochure for the program, an email invitation to an open house and demonstration, and a publicity poster.

1. List five ways you intend to create "buzz."

2. List five common obstacles to e-learning, and for each explain how you propose to overcome it.

[If you've sought help from your marketing communications department, you're naturally going to describe what they are doing for support and show any samples they have developed for you.]

Sustaining E-Learning (chapter 9)

1. How will we provide feedback to learners and their bosses?

2. How will we handle complaints?

3. How will we assess customer satisfaction?

4. How will we keep our focus on the customer?

5. How will we show our customers that we respect them?

6. Do we plan to use "mystery learners"?

7. How will learners be able to co-create future learning events?

8. Are we setting up a learner council?

9. Are experienced employees to mentor new employees?

10. How will we support the development of communities of practice?

11. How frequently will we provide progress reports to stakeholders?

12. What will be in stakeholder reports?

13. How will we identify or solicit new challenges?

14. How will we monitor satisfaction?

15. How will stakeholders request improvements or additions?

16. Are we setting up a board of advisors or a steering committee?

17. Is professional development of one's direct reports in managers' job descriptions?

18. Have supervisors themselves learned to support and reinforce their subordinates' learning?

19. What HR systems need to be changed?

(continued on page 132)

20. What performance management systems need to be changed?

21. What formal and informal rewards and recognition systems will you leverage?

22. What organizational initiatives will you seek to become part of?

Congratulations! You did it! You have created a comprehensive implementation action plan that embraces sound principles of marketing and change management.

Glossary

Marketing Concepts

Augmented product: What you get by adding services to a basic product, for example, industrial chemicals. One tank car of a given chemical contains exactly the same material as the next. A wise supplier included value-added services such as favorable leasing terms, precise delivery dates, and online order entry. This "augmented" product was clearly superior to the competition's.

Brand: A product's reputation, deserved or not. Branding turns commodities into premium products.

Brand equity: The value of a brand, a function of customer loyalty, reputation, and reach.

Brand identity: What your brand aspires to be.

Brand image: What consumers think of your brand.

Buzz: Term of art from Rosen's *The Anatomy of Buzz.* The sum of all comments about a particular product or company at a certain point in time. This is a broad definition that views everything being communicated about a product as the buzz about it.

Cluetrain Manifesto: "Markets are conversations," begins the in-your-face book about marketing in the era of the Web. Until the Web came along, customers were disenfranchised. Complaints? Who cares? Now, customers who are burned by airlines, restaurants, stores, or their Internet service providers can tell their stories to thousands of others by registering their complaints or offering their opinions online. *The Cluetrain Manifesto* is online at www.cluetrain.com.

Commodity: An undifferentiated product. Synonymous with a product that competes only on price.

Lifestyle segmentation: Breaking the market into groups according to their stage in life. For example, a financial services company might think of its market as consisting of students/singles, young married, prime of life, and retirees.

Lifetime customer value: It's unwise to assess the worth of a customer year by year. A college student who opens a checking account may be worth tens of thousands of dollars in fees over time. Because it's cheaper to keep an existing customer than to recruit a new one, improving customer loyalty by investing in customers is generally a good idea.

Market segmentation: Dividing the market into pieces you plan to treat differently. A segment can be almost any group you can identify. For example, in e-learning, meaningful segments might be: centrally located or remote learners, new hires or veterans, sales or service, employees or dealers, executives or front-line supervisor, C++ programmers or Web team, English-speakers or Spanish-speakers, intranet-accessible or outside the firewall.

Market share: Your customers as a percentage of the total market. May be expressed in terms of body count, membership, purchasing, share of sales.

Niche marketing: Target marketing to a small segment, usually mining the veins of rich ore or picking the low-hanging fruit.

Packaging: Brand identity, icon, colors presented consistently so that the product is easily recognized.

Perceived product: What the customer buys. Customers rarely buy commodities. They see a package. They imagine a capability. They find things that meet their needs. They buy a potential emotional payoff.

Positioning: Placing a product in relationship to other products; usually mental rather than physical.

Product: What you offer customers, be they internal or external. Marketers use product in the broadest sense possible. A product could be a physical product, an intangible, a service, a hybrid, or an offer.

Pull strategy: Spend a lot on promotion to "pull" customers into a store to ask for a product.

Push strategy: Use the salesforce and channels to promote the product so that salespeople will "push" it on consumers.

Target market: The group you seek to serve. You can't please all of the people all of the time, so you invest your resources where you expect the greatest return.

Tipping point: From Malcolm Tidwell's book of the same name. A phenomenon that smolders out of sight, then suddenly blazes out of control. Imagine a virus outbreak. A marketing lesson is that a small number of people can make or break a product because they have incredible reach.

CHANGE MANAGEMENT CONCEPTS

Change agent: An informal leader with strong communication, facilitation, and training skills who assists the change process from within the organizational structures.

Communication: A process in which individuals create and share information with one another in order to reach mutual understanding; includes dialogue.

Critical issue: Those issues that are deemed important to the organization, with regard to its present and future performance, and also to its stakeholders.

Critical success factors: A set of factors that are essential to the organization for gaining and maintaining a competitive advantage.

Developmental change: The hierarchically lowest type of organizational change. Limited to improvements on what currently exists. Examples include team building, most quality improvement efforts, enhancing internal communications, increasing technical expertise or core competencies, or basic expansion of services and products. (See also transitional change and transformational change.)

Diffusion of innovations: A theory that analyzes, as well as helps explain, the adaptation of a new innovation. It helps to explain the process of social change.

Effectiveness: Related to outcomes. A measure of the ability of a program, project, or work task to produce a specific desired effect or result that can be qualitatively measured and determined to be better.

Efficiency: Related to resources saved or expended. Refers to operating a program or project, or performing work tasks economically.

Leader: The person or persons who create the vision for change, communicate it clearly, lead by example, and are responsible for ensuring that the change process is linked to the organization.

Mission statement: A statement of the role, or purpose, by which an organization intends to serve its stakeholders. Describes what the organization does (current capabilities), whom it serves (stakeholders), and what makes the organization unique (justification for existence). (See also stakeholder and vision statement.)

Stakeholder: Those individuals, groups, and parties that either affect or who are affected by the organization. Stakeholders, as a general rule, include all internal and external customers. Stakeholders are involved or consulted as a part of the strategic planning process so that their views, needs, and concerns are given consideration during development of organizational goals, objectives, and strategies, and also to provide input related to programmatic outcome measures.

Transformational change: The hierarchically highest of the three types of organizational change. Involves implementation of an evolutionary new state, which requires major and often ongoing shifts in organizational strategy to produce competitive advantage. Examples include reengineering, major restructuring, major shifts in business focus and innovation. (See also transitional change and developmental change.)

Transition: The natural process of moving from an existing state of being to a new state of being, typically through a neutral state.

Transitional change: A type of change that falls in the middle of the three hierarchical types of organizational change. Involves implementation of a new state, which requires dismantling the present ways of operating and introducing new or replacement ways of operating. Examples include reorganization, minor restructuring, utilization of new operational techniques/methods/procedures, or introduction of new services or products. (See also developmental change and transformational change.)

Values: Set of beliefs or standards that the organization (i.e., organizational values) and its stakeholders (i.e., personal values) believe in and operate from. Organizational values guide day-to-day operations, serving as a linkage between mission (i.e., present operations) and vision (i.e., intended direction). Personal values allow organizational members to understand how their own beliefs fit into the organizational values and its intended operations and direction.

Vision statement: Identifies where the organization intends to be in the future or where it should be to best meet the needs of stakeholders. Incorporates a shared understanding of the nature and purpose of the organization and uses this understanding to move the organization toward a greater purpose. (See also mission statement and stakeholder.)

References

ASTD and the MASIE Center. (2001, June). "E-Learning: 'If We Build It, Will They Come?'" http://www.astd.org/virtual_community/research/pdf/844-16110pdf.pdf.

Aaker, J. (1995). "Conceptualizing and Measuring Brand Personality: A Brand Personality Scale." In Aaker, D.A. (1996). *Building Strong Brands.* New York: Simon and Schuster.

Berry, L.L. (1999). *Discovering the Soul of Service: The Nine Drivers of Sustainable Business Success.* New York: The Free Press.

Bridges, W. (1991). *Managing Transitions: Making the Most of Change.* Reading, MA: Addison-Wesley Publishing Company.

Clemente, M.L. (1992). *The Marketing Glossary.* New York: AMACOM Books.

Conner, D.R. (1993). *Managing at the Speed of Change.* New York: Villard Books.

Cross, J., and Q. Clark. (2002). "Meta-Matters: The Value of Learning About Learning." In: *Transforming Culture: An Executive Briefing on the Power of Learning.* Charlottesville, VA: The Batten Institute at the Darden Graduate School of Business Administration. www.meta-learninglab.com.

Davis, S., and C. Meyer. (1998). *Blur: The Speed of Change in the Connected Economy.* Cambridge, MA: Perseus Books.

Gladwell, M. (2000). *The Tipping Point: How Little Things Can Make a Big Difference.* Boston, New York, and London: Little, Brown and Company.

Hammer, M. (1990, April). Presentation at the Index Institute.

Horton, W. (2001). *Evaluating E-Learning.* Alexandria, VA: ASTD.

Jaffe, D.T., and C.D. Scott. (1995). *Managing Change at Work: Leading People Through Organizational Transitions.* Menlo Park, CA: Crisp Publications.

Knowles, M.S. (1990). *The Adult Learner: A Neglected Species.* Houston, TX: Gulf Publishing.

Kotler, P. (1999). *Kotler on Marketing: How to Create, Win, and Dominate Markets.* New York: Free Press.

Kotter, J.P. (1996). *Leading Change.* Boston: Harvard Business School Press.

Langer, E. (1990). *Mindfulness.* Cambridge, MA: Perseus Books.

Langer, E. (1998). *The Power of Mindful Learning.* Cambridge, MA: Perseus Books.

Levinson, J. (1999). *The Truth About Customers.* http://www.gmarketing.com/tactics/weekly.html.

Locke, C., R. Levine, D. Searls, and D. Weinberger. (2001). *The Cluetrain Manifesto: The End of Business as Usual.* Cambridge, MA: Perseus Books. See also www.cluetrain.com.

McKenna, R. (1991, January–February). "Marketing is Everything." *Harvard Business Review,*

McKenna, R. (2002). *Total Access.* Boston: Harvard Business School Press.

Moore, G.A. (2000). *Living on the Fault Line: Managing for Shareholder Value in the Age of the Internet.* New York: HarperBusiness.

Ogilvy, D. (1974). In Caples, J. (1974). *Tested Advertising Methods* (fourth edition). Boston: Reward Books.

Packard, D. (1989). "The Marketing Audit Comes of Age." *Sloan Management Review, 40:* 49–62.

Peters, T., R.H. Waterman, and T. Peters. (1988). *In Search of Excellence: Lessons from America's Best-Run Companies.* New York: Warner Books.

Ries, A., and J. Trout (1994). *The 22 Immutable Laws of Marketing: Violate Them at Your Own Risk.* New York: HarperBusiness.

Ries, A., and L. Ries. (1998). *The 22 Immutable Laws of Branding: How to Build a Product or Service Into a World-Class Brand.* New York: HarperBusiness.

Rogers, E.M. (1995). *The Diffusion of Innovations* (fourth edition). London and New York: MacMillan and Free Press.

Rosen, E. (2000). *Anatomy of Buzz: How to Create Word-Of-Mouth Marketing.* New York: Doubleday.

Roth, H. (2001, August), "Wielding a Brand Name." *Latin CEO.* http://www.landor.com/branding/?action=showArticle&storyid=222.

Smith, J.W., and A. Clurman. (1997). *Rocking the Ages: The Yankelovich Report on Generational Marketing.* New York: HarperCollins.

Tapscott, D. (1998). *Growing Up Digital: The Rise of the Net Generation.* New York: McGraw-Hill.

Trout, J. (2000). *Differentiate or Die.* New York: John Wiley & Sons.

Wilson, L., and S. Johnson. (1986). *The One Minute Sales Person.* Allston, MA: Newman Communications.

About the Authors

Jay Cross has been passionate about harnessing technology to improve adult learning since the 1960s. Fresh out of college, he sold mainframe computers the size of Chevrolet Suburbans. Later, he designed the University of Phoenix's first business degree program. He took a training startup to national prominence, capturing 80 percent market share and training a million professionals to make sound decisions and sell services.

Jay founded Internet Time Group in early 1998 to help organizations learn by providing hands-on advice on implementing e-learning, developing information architecture, advising management, and accelerating sales. Internet Time Group coaches corporate executives on getting the most from their investments in e-learning and collaboration. More than 15,000 people visit www.InternetTime.com every month for e-learning information.

Jay is also CEO of E-Learning Forum, a 1,000-member think tank and advocacy group in Silicon Valley. Jay was principal marketing advisor to CBT Systems during its transition to SmartForce, The eLearning Company. He helped Cisco E-Learning Partners plan, implement, and market their initial Web-based certification programs. He cowrote the vision paper that kicked off the ASTD/National Governors Association Committee on Technology and Adult Learning; contributed a chapter to the recent book *Implementing E-Learning Solutions* (ASTD, 2001); and assisted the Institute for the Future in building global corporate learning scenarios circa 2008.

He is a much sought-after speaker and has written articles for *LINEZine, Learning Circuits, Training & Development, Technology for Learning,* and *American Banker.* Jay is a graduate of Princeton University and Harvard Business School.

Reach him at www.InternetTime.com.

Lance Dublin has been an advocate for innovative approaches to learning and change throughout his career. He went from designing a weeklong "Experiment in Free Form Education" program in high school to cofounding one of the nation's first fully accredited "universities without walls." Then, recognizing the influence of new user-centered technologies on people, business, and learning, he founded and built a company that became a leader in improving individual and organizational performance and implementing large-scale change.

Lance is now an independent consultant based in San Francisco, California. He specializes in corporate learning and change management. His emphasis is in strategy development, program design, and change implementation. He brings to his work more than 30 years' experience in adult education and training, communication and change leadership, and motivation and innovation.

Lance is a nationally recognized authority in:

- developing organizational strategies for the use and implementation of new learning and performance technologies
- creating programs to improve individual and organizational performance (such as e-learning programs, integrated performance support systems, knowledge sharing, and organizational learning systems)
- designing approaches to enable organizations to successfully implement large-scale organizational change (such as new technology-based systems including e-learning programs and ERP, new business processes, new organizational structures, mergers and acquisitions).

Lance is also a highly respected speaker, workshop leader, and author. He has presented at regional, national, and international conferences for organizations such as ASTD, ISPI, VNU Learning, the MASIE Center, Influent Technology Group, and Advanstar.

Lance was president and CEO of Dublin Group from its formation in 1983 until he sold the company in 1998. Under his leadership, this company became recognized for its innovative solutions to improving individual and organizational performance and effective approaches to successfully implementing large-scale change initiatives. Dublin Group's clients included *Fortune* 1,000 clients from across a wide range of industries. Prior to this, Lance was the founder, dean, and later provost of Antioch University/West, an innovative accredited bachelor's and master's degree program serving a thousand students in the western states and Hawaii.

You may contact Lance via email at ldublin@pacbell.net.

The Value of Belonging

ASTD membership keeps you up to date on the latest developments in your field, and provides top-quality, *practical* information to help you stay ahead of trends, polish your skills, measure your progress, demonstrate your effectiveness, and advance your career.

We give you what you need most from the entire scope of workplace learning and performance:

Information

We're your best resource for research, best practices, and background support materials – the data you need for your projects to excel.

Networking

We're the facilitator who puts you in touch with colleagues, experts, field specialists, and industry leaders – the people you need to know to succeed.

Technology

We're the clearinghouse for new technologies in training, learning, and knowledge management in the workplace – the background you need to stay ahead.

Analysis

We look at cutting-edge practices and programs and give you a balanced view of the latest tools and techniques – the understanding you need on what works and what doesn't.

Competitive Edge

ASTD is your leading resource on the issues and topics that are important to you. That's the value of belonging!

For more information, or to become a member, please call 1.800.628.2783 (U.S.) or +1.703.683.8100; visit our website at **www.astd.org**; or send an email to customercare@astd.org.

Linking People,
Learning & Performance

31410d

Printed in the United States
102440LV00002B/51-150/A

9 781562 863333